Urban Crisis, Urban Hope

Anthem Environment and Sustainability Initiative

The Anthem Environment and Sustainability Initiative (AESI) seeks to push the frontiers of scholarship while simultaneously offering prescriptive and programmatic advice to policymakers and practitioners around the world. The programme publishes research monographs, professional and major reference works, upper-level textbooks and general interest titles. Professor Lawrence Susskind, as General Editor of AESI, oversees the below book series, each with its own series editor and an editorial board featuring scholars, practitioners and business experts keen to link theory and practice.

Strategies for Sustainable Development Series

Series Editor: Professor Lawrence Susskind (MIT)
Climate Change Science, Policy and Implementation

Series Editor: Dr. Brooke Hemming (US EPA)
Science Diplomacy: Managing Food, Energy and Water Sustainably

Series Editor: Professor Shafiqul Islam (Tufts University)
International Environmental Policy Series

Series Editor: Professor Saleem Ali (University of Delaware)
Big Data and Sustainable Cities Series

Series Editor: Professor Sarah Williams (MIT)
Climate Change and the Future of the North American City

Series Editor: Richardson Dilworth
(Center for Public Policy, Drexel University, USA)

Included within the AESI is the Anthem EnviroExperts Review. Through this online micro-review site, Anthem Press seeks to build a community of practice involving scientists, policy analysts and activists committed to creating a clearer and deeper understanding of how ecological systems – at every level – operate, and how they have been damaged by unsustainable development. This site publishes short reviews of important books or reports in the environmental field, broadly defined. Visit the website: www.anthemenviroexperts.com.

Urban Crisis, Urban Hope

A Policy Agenda for UK Cities

Edited by

Julian Dobson and Rowland Atkinson

ANTHEM PRESS

Anthem Press
An imprint of Wimbledon Publishing Company
www.anthempress.com

This edition first published in UK and USA 2020
by ANTHEM PRESS
75–76 Blackfriars Road, London SE1 8HA, UK
or PO Box 9779, London SW19 7ZG, UK
and
244 Madison Ave #116, New York, NY 10016, USA

© 2020 Julian Dobson and Rowland Atkinson editorial matter and selection;
individual chapters © individual contributors

The moral right of the authors has been asserted.

All rights reserved. Without limiting the rights under copyright reserved above,
no part of this publication may be reproduced, stored or introduced into
a retrieval system, or transmitted, in any form or by any means
(electronic, mechanical, photocopying, recording or otherwise),
without the prior written permission of both the copyright
owner and the above publisher of this book.

British Library Cataloguing-in-Publication Data
A catalogue record for this book is available from the British Library.

ISBN-13: 978-1-78527-468-8 (Hbk)
ISBN-10: 1-78527-468-6 (Hbk)
ISBN-13: 978-1-78527-471-8 (Pbk)
ISBN-10: 1-78527-471-6 (Pbk)

This title is also available as an e-book.

CONTENTS

Acknowledgements		vii
Foreword by Leo Hollis, Author of Cities Are Good for You		ix
Chapter 1.	Asking for Trouble *Julian Dobson and Rowland Atkinson*	1
Chapter 2.	The Hungry City	11
	A Growing Resistance to Britain's Food Poverty Crisis *Madeleine Power*	11
	What Will It Take to End Hunger in the United Kingdom? *Niall Cooper*	17
Chapter 3.	The Unhomed City	23
	Housing Crisis, Austerity and the Production of Precarious Lives *Emma Bimpson and Richard Goulding*	23
	Council Housing in the Urban Mixer *Glyn Robbins*	29
Chapter 4.	The Anxious City	37
	Rediscovering 'We-ness' *Rhiannon Corcoran*	37
	The Anxious City Is a Complicated Place *Graham Marshall*	43
Chapter 5.	The Violent City	49
	Violence in the City: Inequality, Intimidation and Fear *Elizabeth Cook and Anthony Ellis*	49
	Mattering and the Violence in Our Cities *Luke Billingham and Keir Irwin-Rogers*	55

Chapter 6.	The Sick City	63
	Do Black Lives Matter in Polluted Cities? *Bethany Thompson*	63
	Growing Our Way to Healthier Cities *Pam Warhurst*	68
Chapter 7.	The Withering City	75
	How Can We Save and Restore Our Urban Green Spaces? *Ian Mell*	75
	Cities Can Be Green Havens *Natalie Bennett*	81
Chapter 8.	The Dispossessed City	87
	Dispossession through Gentrification *Loretta Lees*	87
	Land and Displacement *Kate Swade and Mark Walton*	93
Chapter 9.	The Unravelling City	101
	Facing the Public Services Crisis *Annette Hastings*	101
	Resisting the New Normal *Julian Dobson*	107
Chapter 10.	The Unaccountable City	113
	An Unfinished Democracy *Simin Davoudi*	113
	Does Urban Government Have to Be Destructive? *Jess Steele*	119
Chapter 11.	The Challenge of Change *Rowland Atkinson and Julian Dobson*	127
Chapter 12.	A Manifesto for Urban Policy	129
List of Contributors		135
Index		137

ACKNOWLEDGEMENTS

This book emerged from conversations in 2017 and an associated event on how Sheffield could become a better city. It quickly became clear that while our own city of Sheffield has a particular set of urban problems, the absence of urban policy at a national level in the United Kingdom and the complacency of central government towards local democracy and local public services are affecting all urban areas to different degrees. Here we would like to acknowledge the contributions of the many who have taken part in the conversations that have shaped this book, and those who took part in the Sheffield event that sparked this process.

FOREWORD

There is an old joke about asking for directions. A person is driving through the countryside and comes to a village and stops to ask a man if he knows how to get to 'X'. The man thinks about it for a bit and then answers: 'Yes, I know how to get there, but if I were you, I wouldn't start from here.' Except, of course, we have no choice. And it is getting late. And we are running out of petrol. And the passengers in the back are thirsty. And a slow sense of panic is starting to set in. No one would start from here, if they had a choice; but here we are.

As I am sitting down to write, the air that encircles Delhi has turned toxic. The city has poisoned itself. Two weeks ago in Santiago, Chile, protesters torched metro stations following a fare hike on the public transport system. In Hong Kong, each Saturday, the streets are filled in defiance of a growing surveillance state that uses the infrastructure of the city to unblinkingly watch over its citizens. The latest addition to the Manhattan skyline is Hudson Yards, a bland, shiny enclave surmounted by Thomas Heatherwick's empty icon, the Vessel, that prides itself on being the most quantified space in New York. Closer to home, in London, there are more homeless people on the streets than in living memory. We are stressed out. Divided. Fearful of both violence and the police. Our neoliberal chickens are settling into their urban roost.

But, didn't we all – as urbanists, human geographers, sociologists, historians and policy thinkers – start our fascination with the urban world because we thought that there was something different, perhaps even liberating, about city life? And, despite the desperate reality on the ground today, didn't we share a feeling that the urban realm could be a place of nurture, of flourishing? We study the current problems, their origins and mutations, so that one might one day change them. We acknowledge that while the city is home to, and even multiplier of, many of the horrors of the conjuncture we find ourselves, it is also the crucible of its remedy. Is this enough to discern a glimmer of hope?

In the varied, engaged entries in this collection that explore the many violences that urban life bestows upon its citizens, the ecosystem and our planet, a throbbing, repetitive call and response reverberates: 'Who is the city for?' it questions; 'Not you!' the echo replies. The collective portrait these chapters paint is of a metropolis stripped of its citizenry. A place that denies belonging. A street filled with bodies but devoid of civic life. The neoliberal city is a financial instrument, calibrated for profit above all things. Everything is assigned an exchange value. Everyday life is the stuff of arbitrage.

What is to be done?

Rest assured: the city was here before capital turned the metropolis into an exchange, and will remain long after it has gone. But we cannot put our hope in 'hope' itself. As the extensive catalogue of tasks to be assigned in the final chapter show, there is much to be done. A city that is made of people, that is structured for the flourishing of each of us, and that sits gently on the earth is a job of work rather than wishing. It involves small, daily changes as well as global, singular disruptions. This book sets out on the first steps of this task, and is most welcome; in fact, it is utterly necessary and urgent.

Leo Hollis

Leo Hollis is a historian and urbanist. He has written two historical books on London: *The Phoenix* and *The Stones of London,* as well as the international bestseller *Cities Are Good for You: The Genius of the Metropolis*. He is currently working on a history of land and London. He works in publishing and lives in London. Twitter: @leohollis

Chapter 1

ASKING FOR TROUBLE

Julian Dobson and Rowland Atkinson

To talk of hope today is to ask for trouble.

It is asking for trouble in the traditional sense of the phrase: the hopes we express frequently evaporate in the glare of reality, or return to bite us. We live in an era where hopes of equality and of better places to live in have been dashed time and again, most recently by the impacts of austerity and precarity, and where belief in progressive, evidence-based policies is frequently shouted down by a politics of blame or boosterism, or the demands of more immediate crises.

But the idea of hope also asks for trouble in a more literal sense. To express hope and to translate hope into demands and propositions for change is to trouble and disturb taken-for-granted ways of doing things. Serious hope will provoke opposition. It threatens existing systems and structures, many of which now thrive on inequality and insecurity.

Yet such systems and structures are increasingly shown to be incapable of functioning or providing effectively in troubled times. The COVID-19 pandemic of spring 2020, which was still accelerating at the time of writing, underlined such incapacities starkly. In cities around the world, and in the United Kingdom in particular, the onrush of coronavirus has, more than any ideological or political challenge, exposed the failings of urban economies and the stripping out of state capacity, alongside the privileging of market actors and their beneficiaries. Our cities have been revealed as places where swathes of the population working in the gig economy can lose their livelihoods at short notice; where government has been compelled to prevent the eviction of private renters; but where the food banks that have stepped in to plug gaping holes in the welfare safety net are forced to close as older volunteers are quarantined, or are left dependent on the generosity of supermarket bosses. The sudden cessation of much everyday activity has also exposed the levels of ambient pollution urban dwellers must endure: suddenly, in many areas, the air has become more breathable and the natural world can be seen and heard. What this crisis emphasised, like a rapidly withdrawing tide, was the ugly shape of contemporary inequalities. In the spaces of our cities could be seen the key dividing lines – between asset-rich owners and landlords, on the one hand, and poorer tenants, on the other. More broadly, the disconnect could be seen between those operating the suddenly much less exciting gig economy and those with waged positions; between young and old; and between residents of spacious or higher-quality housing, and the many now living in high-rise, poorly designed or badly maintained rented homes.

These examples point to a deepening crisis, often overseen and unchallenged by an unwilling or antagonistic central state apparatus that is deeply aligned with the demands of capital and much less with the communities that its policies have, in many cases, quite clearly damaged. It is a crisis that will continue until we collectively acknowledge the need to rebuild the foundational infrastructure of our cities – the urban spaces and social glue that enable our communities to thrive.

Hope demands the apparently impossible in order to reveal what could be. It asserts that current configurations fall short, and poses the question of how a better future can be attained. In the same breath it expresses discontent and optimism. Working with these possibilities, this volume seeks to highlight a series of troubles in our cities today, but also to offer clear and practical steps that could be instigated to redress them. Our mandate derives from an enormous absence. This gap is defined by the lack of state supports and policy programmes that could and should be designed to alleviate the worst spatial and social features of capitalism (uneven development, pockets of poverty, disinvestment in core services and housing, among many others). For over a decade we have seen our cities devitalised and damaged by an absence of action or interest from central government, coupled with a meekness and despair among many local authorities as their budgets have been slashed in half.

Hope views reality through a critical lens, but it is not a dead criticality: it is alive with possibility, and with the urgency of change. It counters the temptation to despair by insisting that another world is possible. In the famous words of Arundhati Roy, hope allows us to 'hear her breathing'. Hope does not simply wish that things were different, but proposes and agitates and listens for that difference. It is grounded in the history and practice of change, of rights won and goals achieved – from universal suffrage to legislation on air quality, from accessible healthcare to basic housing standards. It recognises that those struggles are unfinished and historic achievements cannot be taken for granted. If anything these possibilities feel all the more palpable *because* of the crisis our cities endure today.

The ecological crisis will ultimately switch citizens and consumers en masse away from a fossil-fuel urban economy, with massive ramifications for economies, transport systems, housing construction and adaptation, and consumption of goods and services. The yawning chasm of wealth inequality framed around property ownership or its absence has given momentum to ideas to decommodify and build municipal housing. Meanwhile, in the area of governance, enormous deficits in the need for local accountability and resources are constantly yielding innovations in how local economies and polities can be rebuilt.

But if these are general characteristics of hope, what does a specifically *urban* hope look like? And what does it look like in the peculiarly troubled context of the United Kingdom? This book arises from our interests, and those of the various contributors, in urban policy and practice – in what happens in the complex networks of people, things and activities that we label towns and cities.

Why an *Urban* Hope?

In this collection we view cities as the epicentre of social damage and trauma that have unwound over generations and intensified under conditions of public sector decimation in the past decade. But we also suggest that we must look to the city as the most likely arena for these and other challenges to be resolved. Policies that do not work for cities miss most of humanity: both at a global scale, with more than half the world's population now living in cities, and particularly in the United Kingdom, where nine-tenths of the population live in urban areas. Cities starkly reflect social inequalities: in Sheffield, where the editors of this book work, there is a difference in life expectancy of nearly ten years between those living at one end of the city's 83 bus route and the other. These disparities are encountered all around the United Kingdom's urban centres, places of wealth and poverty, health and personal deterioration, educational excellence and developmental stasis and neglect. These facts are not evidence of a rich tapestry of city life. They highlight places that exemplify and build inequality, forms of injustice that stand no test of basic fairness or principles of common purpose.

Cities generate stresses. In many ways they both produce and receive the challenges of climate change, creating enormous demands for raw materials and energy, exacerbating flooding through large areas of hard surfacing and experiencing intensifying heatwaves among densely packed buildings. Cities highlight the strains of governance and local politics, as institutions seek to deliver services under financial constraints while politicians and new power blocs compete for domination. Urban life is where the impacts of austerity bite hardest, from the seemingly exponential growth of food banks in the last decade to the increasing numbers of rough sleepers on urban streets and the disabled people who are further disadvantaged by withdrawals of financial and service supports. Cities are also sites of an enduring reliance on a limited offer of escapism and self-harm, notably the violence and enormous financial cost of alcohol-fuelled night-time urban economies and the many nights at accident and emergency units at urban hospitals that ensue. These pressures highlight our cities as places of tensions and unresolved action to create more cohesive spaces that respond to environmental and human needs for flourishing outside a narrow reliance on consumption, whether of clothes, cars, energy or alcohol.

Cities are where people's sense of belonging and identity may be tested by demographic and social change, and where what Doreen Massey calls the 'thrown-togetherness' of place can often also feel like a kind of pulling apart of the social fabric. Today's urban context is particularly characterised by precarity: insecurity of work, income, health, housing and insecurity within the natural and built environment, from run-down parks where people fear to go, to the wider insecurities of climate change and biodiversity loss. Precarity is not unique to cities, but it can be more extreme, more concentrated and starker in contrast with the wealth and privilege continually thrust in the face of urban dwellers. The contributors to this book highlight in different ways the extent and consequences of that precarity, from the child in Lewisham whose death was directly linked with the polluted air of her neighbourhood, to the thousands of parents of young children who face five weeks without income after their first Universal Credit income support claim. Here it seems telling that the UK government's stubborn reluctance to loosen the strictures of Universal Credit began to waver in the face of the reality check brought on by COVID-19.

Precarity and Possibility

Two decades ago the author Rebecca Solnit wrote the first of the essays that were compiled in her collection, *Hope in the Dark*. In her introduction she writes that 'to hope is to gamble. It's to bet on the future, on your desires, on the possibility that an open heart and uncertainty is better than gloom and safety.' The authors who have come together in this book are united in that wager. They arrive at this bet on possibility from different perspectives and disciplines, different careers and different politics. But all are convinced our cities can be better, and can become the foundation for a thriving and flourishing society. Each of them has included in their contributions an agenda for action: achievable changes that with sufficient will and application can begin now. Taken together, they show how urban policy, politics and, indeed, community or individual action may be re-energised and form a catalyst for change with positive consequences well beyond the urban fringes. Crucially, their recommendations are grounded in experience and observation of what is happening in our cities now – not only the manifestations of crisis, but also the promise of solutions embedded in community-based action and embodied in the actions of urban dwellers who hold out their hands to feed people who are hungry, plant seeds in unpromising corners and start conversations with neighbours.

These recommendations in different ways address the challenge of precarity. Precarity is not the same as persistent poverty, although people who are persistently poor face it most brutally. Precarity is the condition of an increasing proportion of people who never imagined that they would be poor or unable to cope with urban life. Take Emma, the Cambridge mother of three children described by Niall Cooper in Chapter 2, who in the space of six months moved from a £30,000 job in human resources to having to rely on food charity. People in Emma's position don't expect to live precarious lives, but find a change in circumstances can lead to a downward spiral of hardship.

Precarity affects the physical environment too: Ian Mell describes the neglect of parks and green spaces in Chapter 7, and Jess Steele notes in Chapter 10 the process of 'watching beams rot' as irresponsible or incapable ownership takes its toll on the urban fabric. These examples highlight the need for a more compassionate and empathic treatment of urban poverty, an imaginary of support that understands how risks and traumas can visit almost anyone's life. But we must also understand the need for greater equality, social justice and support where the cleavages of class, geography, ethnicity and region intersect to produce evident and enduring forms of social damage. It is in response to these conditions that the state should be intervening and helping, rather than withdrawing, as many of the contributions here observe. We see this withdrawal in numerous areas of social policy with spatial consequences, including Universal Credit and housing benefit, and the almost total loss of spatially targeted state support, including housing, urban and regional policy.

Urban centres are intersections of multiple forms of precarity, which often combine to tip individuals and families from coping into crisis. Food poverty is one of the most striking, because of the speed with which food banks and similar forms of crisis assistance have become normalised as the traditional welfare safety net disintegrates – and the vulnerability of that system of crisis assistance in the face of wider shocks such as COVID-19. Secure housing, once regarded as a right, is now out of the reach of a growing percentage of the population: as a recent report from housing experts at the University of York detailed, 27 per cent of private rented homes in England fail to meet decency standards, while there is growing evidence of a 'shadow' rental market characterised by 'very high levels of criminality [...] trafficking and drug dealing'.[1] Even housing benefit itself has become a form of state support for private landlordism, where in many cases private profit for some is underpinned by private squalor for others.

Less physically obvious than the challenges of food poverty and housing insecurity is the precarity of mental health. An increasingly stressed and anxious population is less able to cope with other challenges: mental ill-health and the material trials of low income or poor housing reinforce each other. As Graham Marshall comments in Chapter 4, 'You shouldn't measure a city by its richest street, but by its poorest.' His sobering conclusion is that by such a yardstick, he cannot think of a good place.

In Chapter 5 we turn to the violence, and fear of violence, which also characterises many urban lives. Physical violence is sometimes the most extreme end of the spectrum of precarity: it is those who live the most precarious lives who most often become the victims of violence. Our cities, as Luke Billingham and Keir Irwin-Rogers highlight, persistently tell our young people that they don't matter.

While violence is specific and personal, there are also general factors that make urban lives more precarious, especially in poorer neighbourhoods. Bethany Thompson underlines how the risks of poor air quality fall disproportionately on Black and minority populations, who are less likely to have the resources to move from areas permeated by pollution and fumes. Natalie Bennett shows how poor planning and ignorant practices continue to destroy the biodiversity of our cities – places that could instead become havens for wildlife.

Our assertion in this book is that precarity is not simply a fact of life in poverty, but is a condition of urban life that increasingly affects all but the wealthiest, and has been brought about by a sustained erosion of the physical and social support required for urban life. But while cities are places of challenge, they are simultaneously places of possibility. They are the places where it is often easier for like-minded people to work together to address common challenges, creating housing cooperatives or community gardens, sharing cultural festivals and supporting people who are ill or distressed. They are places where it is possible to rediscover what Rhiannon Corcoran, in Chapter 4, describes as 'lives well-lived and enjoyed […] places of meaning and purpose'.

The Contributions

This collection tackles themes of precarity and possibility in our cities, moving from issues that are predominantly felt at an individual scale to collective challenges of how we service and govern our cities. In all cases our contributors challenge the binary of the atomised individual and the unyielding bureaucracy, showing that collective and communal solutions and actions can bring a sense of agency and hope to people who feel powerless and institutions that have been disempowered. Each chapter offers two 'takes' on the urban crisis: the reader is given a 'macro' analytical statement by academic researchers drawing on the latest knowledge in their field. This is supplemented by the view of established practitioners and observers offering a grounded framing of the issues from their perspective and experiences. The benefit of this approach becomes clear as we step between strategic, but often more abstracted, framings of the issues, to those built from a relationship to the frontline of practice.

Chapter 2 begins with a crisis felt at the most personal level, detailing how times of hardship are increasingly times of hunger. Madeleine Power and Niall Cooper describe how this has spawned a growing network of community-based food organisations – including, increasingly, groups that are committed to ending the dependence on food banks and restoring dignity to those who use them.

In Chapter 3 we turn to a set of issues that in many ways define the urban crisis. Here Emma Bimpson and Richard Goulding consider the long-standing problems of homelessness and a lack of decent housing for those in need. They argue for a renewed interest in housing by the state and greater commitments to public housing. These positions are echoed and reinforced by the view from an estate in central London, narrated by Glyn Robbins in relation to what he sees as new forms of ownership, exclusion and transience opened up by continuing forms of privatisation and housing inequality in the city.

Chapter 4 addresses the anxiety that has become a backdrop to urban life for many. Rhiannon Corcoran calls for a rebuilding of the social networks that make cities liveable, while Graham Marshall considers what places would look like if urban systems such as transport networks were designed to enable people to thrive and flourish. They call for a new emphasis on the social networks and emotional attachments that build place and community, putting social sustainability centre stage.

In Chapter 5 Lizzie Cook and Tony Ellis offer an incisive analysis of the key mechanisms of state withdrawal and increasing inequality now shaping problems of violence in our towns and cities. Picking up this theme from close engagement with young people in London, Luke Billingham and Keir Irwin-Rogers consider how the urban crisis framed around violence is, in reality, rooted in forms of alienation and a breakdown in meaning and self-worth for many young people, enormously amplified by the withdrawal of resources from many urban communities.

The notion of the sick city is tackled in Chapter 6, with a focus on two particular public health challenges: air quality and healthy food. Bethany

Thompson exposes the discriminatory effects of air pollution, asking whether Black lives really matter in polluted urban environments. Pam Warhurst highlights the lack of effective action to address public health challenges and shows how the Incredible Edible movement has inspired people to take the opportunity themselves to begin to change food systems, bringing together community, learning and business in a quest for a kinder way of life.

The wider natural environment is the focus of Chapter 7. Ian Mell calls for new thinking on the future of parks and urban green spaces that have been subject to disproportionate cuts under austerity regimes, while Natalie Bennett makes the case for cities to become havens of biodiversity, underpinned by improved planning and transport systems. While they make a strong case for reversing public sector cuts, both contributors look forward to new approaches to the natural urban environment rather than harking back to an imagined golden age of green investment.

In Chapter 8 Loretta Lees considers how demolition and state action promoting gentrification have led to wholesale and significant housing dispossession, particularly in cities like London. Kate Swade and Mark Walton meanwhile offer an engaging analysis of inequalities of land ownership and how the increasing privatisation of public space underlines the urgent need for new thinking and reform to make our cities happier and more humane.

Chapter 9 focuses on how the disintegration and dismantling of public services is fraying the social bonds that arise from shared experiences and participation in society. Annette Hastings details the impact of a decade of cuts and calls for a new conversation about council services, while Julian Dobson challenges a 'new normal' of low expectations, cuts and closures and calls for the empowerment encapsulated in the idea of a universal income to be matched with the stability guaranteed by universal basic services.

In Chapter 10 Simin Davoudi and Jess Steele highlight the loss of community, and communities' assets, that has arisen from a flawed conception of localism and a destructive mode of urban governance. Simin Davoudi calls urban democracy an unfinished business and urges its revitalisation through more deliberative forms of governance such as citizens' assemblies, while Jess Steele calls on decision-makers to acknowledge and facilitate the self-organised efforts of local communities to protect and improve the places and spaces that matter to them.

Conclusion

Through this collection of essays we invite politicians, policymakers and urban practitioners from all professions and walks of life to engage with us in a critical hope. We suggest such a critical hope will have four salient characteristics.

First, it is clear-sighted. It does not shy away from the enormity of the crisis we face – whether that is manifest in the effects of climate change and the destruction of the natural environment, the abuse and exclusion of groups of people because of their race or gender, or the mounting toll of social policies that generate poverty and homelessness.

Second, it is empathic. It identifies with those who are the victims and losers. It looks for ways to draw alongside them and amplify their voices. A critical hope is angry at the treatment of humans who, by dint of disadvantage, bad luck or deliberate policy, have had hope taken from them. Third, it is creative. It does not take refuge in stale theory or political clichés, but imaginatively uses theory, politics, the arts and practical actions to take action. It does not devalue small contributions because they are inadequate, but views them as seeds of the possible. Finally, a critical hope is stubborn. It persists when the evidence suggests it has made no difference and when the powerful refuse to listen, and it insists on finding ways round, over and in between obstacles. It does not shut up or shut down in the face of opposition.

Hope is not the domain of a particular group or political alignment. It is most powerful when it brings diverse voices together and is open to new and different perspectives, and when it acknowledges the unsung and unnoticed work in which any vision of a better future must be grounded. In bringing a few of these voices together, some familiar and some new, we want to revive hopeful conversations about cities and urban policy that have been stifled for too long. Such conversations are needed now more than ever.

Note

1 J. Rugg and D. Rhodes, 'The Evolving Private Rented Sector: Its Contribution and Potential'. Centre for Housing Policy, 2018. Accessed 7 October 2019. http://www.nationwidefoundation.org.uk/wp-content/uploads/2018/09/Private-Rented-Sector-report.pdf.

Chapter 2

THE HUNGRY CITY

A GROWING RESISTANCE TO BRITAIN'S FOOD POVERTY CRISIS

Madeleine Power

We are in the throes of a crisis of food poverty in the United Kingdom. Between 1 April 2018 and 31 March 2019, the Trussell Trust's network of food banks distributed 1.6 million three-day emergency food supplies to people in crisis, a 19 per cent increase from the previous year and a 26-fold increase from 2010/2011. More than half a million of these food supplies went to children.[1]

These shocking statistics reflect only the tip of the iceberg of food poverty – or food insecurity. Trussell Trust food banks represent roughly two-thirds of all food banks operating in the United Kingdom, and only a minority of all food aid providers. Research by the Independent Food Aid Network and Menu for Change in Scotland found that 221,977 food parcels were distributed by 84 independent food banks operating across Scotland between April 2017 and September 2018, roughly equivalent to the 258,606 emergency food parcels distributed by Trussell Trust food banks.

Food insecurity, the 'limited access to food [...] due to lack of money or financial resources', appears to be at unprecedented levels in the United Kingdom.[2] There is no single, nationwide government measure for food insecurity. Small-scale studies, though, paint a picture of a widespread and urgent food insecurity crisis. A study by the Food Standards Agency found that 13 per cent of adults are 'marginally food secure' and 8 per cent have low or very low food security. Low or very low food security typically means a person going through a whole day without eating at various times during the year because they cannot afford food.[3] A 2018 report by the Food and Agriculture Organisation (FAO), averaging data from 2015 to 2017, estimated that 2.2 million people in the United Kingdom were severely food insecure.[4] This is the highest reported level in Europe, and implies that the United Kingdom is responsible for one in five of all severely food insecure people in Europe. Food insecurity is particularly high among people who are unemployed (47 per cent of whom report food insecurity) and those in the lowest-income quartile (34 per cent). Women are more likely to live in food insecure households than men (10 per cent compared to 6 per cent) and there is evidence that the likelihood of food insecurity varies by ethnic group.[5]

Food insecurity denotes a broad category of experiences, ranging from episodes of acute hunger to concern about the ability to obtain food. So it may be a transitory state, relieved by receiving food from a food bank or from friends and family. But it may also be a chronic experience. Episodes of hunger may be set against a backdrop of permanent concern about affording sufficient food. Parents of young children in York and Bradford describe their constant struggle to afford healthy and fresh food for their children. Here is one typical comment: 'Healthy food is expensive. I often skip meals so that I can afford to feed my children a healthy balanced diet. I expect this is the case in many households.'

Food insecurity or food poverty appears to be a relatively new phenomenon in the United Kingdom, even though poverty itself is persistent. Prior to 2010, both the notion of food insecurity and the existence of food banks were largely unknown. The salience of food insecurity today and, especially, the widespread use of food banks, can largely be attributed to the £30 billion of cuts in working-age social security initiated by the Coalition government in 2010. These cuts are still being rolled out, despite former premier Theresa May's declaration at the 2018 Conservative Party conference that 'austerity is over'. Cuts to working-age social security since 2010 include the abolition of the Health in Pregnancy Grant, the localisation of the Social Fund and the abolition of the School Maintenance Grant.

The value of working-age benefits, for people in and out of work, has been steadily eroded by uprating changes. In 2016, working-age benefits and tax credits – including some for people who are too unwell to work – were frozen until 2020. According to the Joseph Rowntree Foundation, this will affect more than 27 million people and sweep 400,000 into poverty. When the freeze ends in 2020/21, a substantial proportion of the financial saving will have come from the incomes of some of the most vulnerable households in the United Kingdom.

The imposition of local rent limits has reduced the value of Housing Benefit, forcing some tenants to pay a proportion of their rent out of their food budget. The 'bedroom tax' has had a similar effect – tenants in social housing have their benefit reduced by 14 per cent if they have a spare bedroom or 25 per cent if they have two or more. The localisation of Council Tax support has, in effect, forced those receiving working-age social security to pay some or all of their Council Tax – an abrupt and sharp increase in outgoings for households who were previously exempt. Larger families have suffered huge losses from the roll-out of the benefit cap, which limits the total amount of income from certain benefits a household can receive. The two-child limit, which restricts the 'child element' in Universal Credit and tax credits and is worth £2,780 per child per year, to the first two children, has similarly resulted in significant losses for families.

Most detrimentally, the roll-out of the Universal Credit system has precipitated sudden and severe financial losses for many households. Excessive waiting times, delays in receiving payments, debt and loan repayments, and punitive benefit sanctions have rendered many people destitute. The devastating impact on household finances is manifest in countless testimonials of benefit claimants: 'Universal Credit has wrecked us. We have just gone on it and I have been told me and my five-year-old will have to go at least seven weeks with no income at all. We will have to go to food banks and try to get food.'

These changes to working-age social security are directly reflected in rising food bank use. In 2018, the Trussell Trust attributed 24 per cent of its emergency referrals to 'benefit delays' and 18 per cent to 'benefit changes'. It found that, on average, 12 months after Universal Credit roll-out, food banks see a 52 per cent increase in demand, compared with 13 per cent in areas where Universal Credit has been in place for three months or less. This increase exists after accounting for seasonal and other variations, suggesting Universal Credit is a causal factor.

Such cuts have occurred against a backdrop of wider insecurity and inequality: of rising living costs; of low paid and insecure work; and of stagnating wages in the middle of the income range, accompanied by rising incomes at the top. Indeed, low income is the strongest and most consistent predictor of food insecurity – at the local, national and international level.

Poverty rates are rising and, without policy change, this trajectory is forecast to continue. Child poverty is projected to rise by a further 6 percentage points to 29 per cent by 2023–24, which on existing data would mark a record high – even surpassing the highs of the 1990s. Of the factors affecting incomes in the coming years that are relatively clear – those relating to planned policy on minimum wages and benefits – it seems likely that the net impact will be to increase inequality in household incomes.

Beneath these statistics are individual lives of struggle and stress. Parents in York and Bradford describe the anxiety induced by rising food prices and high rent amid stagnant, or falling, incomes. They respond by buying less healthy but cheaper food or using credit cards for food purchases: 'The food is getting more expensive and I am always anxious to go to the shop and see how much I spend as its looks like more all the time. Going to shops creates a lot of stress.

I use a credit card to pay for food and hope I will have enough money to cover it every month.'

Rising poverty and food insecurity erodes community life. It is well established that people living with poverty and food insecurity strategise to avoid the associated stigma at all costs. They may withdraw from social interactions which may expose their poverty, thereby shunning potential forms of social and family support. They may also align themselves with dominant discourses of a 'culture of poverty', distinguishing those deemed socially 'deserving' of state support from those who are 'undeserving'. The insidious effects of such discourses are observed in the social divisions that emerge as individuals attempt to distance themselves from those deemed undeserving of welfare. The 'undeserving' recipient is inextricably linked in the public perception with the person in poverty. Conversations in Bradford made clear that these discourses undermine potential solidarity among women living with food insecurity:

> There is one kid that we know at school and the mum brags that she goes there to get things, 'I don't go food shopping because I just go to food bank.'
>
> I don't know them but I know of them, she's got six kids, she is on Income Support and the baby's dad don't help her at all but she goes out every weekend and she uses the food bank because she ends up spending the money on clothes and beer.

The effects of falling incomes and reduced public assistance are spread unevenly across the United Kingdom, and fall disproportionately on cities. While austerity policy delivered across-the-board budget cuts to almost all government departments, these cuts are harsher in certain areas and to certain services. Analysis of government data by the Institute for Fiscal Studies shows that the largest spending cuts tend to be in cities, such as Liverpool, Manchester, Birmingham and Newcastle. All received a high proportion of their funding from central government before 2010, and experienced cuts of over 25 per cent to total service spending between 2010 and 2015.[6]

In response, some local authorities now only provide the most basic functions and have dropped many preventative interventions. Those with the biggest service spending cuts are withdrawing services the fastest, shifting responsibility for societal well-being towards individuals, the private sector and the third sector.

The civil society response to rising food insecurity and destitution has been swift, widespread and varied. Most noticeably, the Trussell Trust network of food banks has grown rapidly from 12 a year between 2003 and 2008 to roughly 400 food banks operating out of 1,200 food bank centres today – a shocking increase. Alongside Trussell Trust food banks, there exist more than eight hundred 'independent' food banks run by other organisations and an unknown number of other emergency and non-emergency food sources, such as soup kitchens, pay-as-you-feel cafes, community kitchens, community supermarkets and community gardens.

The rapid growth in food banks distributing 'emergency' supplies to people in crisis exemplifies the strength of community commitment and energy to help others in austere times. Whether the proliferation of food banks is a source of hope, however, remains questionable. The 'voucher system', in which food can only be received from the food bank on the condition that an individual presents a 'voucher' accessed from and signed by another service provider, such as a GP, may construct – and cement – a division between those thought deserving of food support and those considered undeserving. The absence of choice undermines the agency of service users and may exacerbate the perceived stigma of food bank use. Service users are given a defined parcel of food, containing a nutritionally balanced diet for up to three days; while some food banks may provide limited choice within or in addition to this parcel, this is not generally the case. More fundamentally, the very existence and expansion of food banks may facilitate further austerity and welfare reform. By accepting responsibility for individual well-being, food banks relieve the state of its responsibility to prevent destitution.

Other forms of food aid may, nevertheless, offer some hope and a sense of the possible. Many food aid organisations avoid the (traditionally) transactional and delimited model of food bank support. For instance, community supermarkets can provide choice, and service users may be valued and respected through involvement in decision-making and governance. Further, many community cafes offer universal, open-access provision – thereby avoiding the stigma associated with means-tested support – and encourage sociability between service users through communal meals.

National organisations and coalitions, including End Hunger UK, Sustain, the Independent Food Aid Network and Menu for Change, campaign on the systemic causes of food poverty and insecurity, including poverty and living costs, welfare reform and debt. They also galvanise and support grassroots alliances to tackle and campaign locally on food poverty. The work of Food Power is particularly noteworthy in this respect. Food Power's financial and expert assistance has supported over sixty-five local alliances addressing food poverty through collaboration, campaigning and local service provision. There has been considerable success in raising awareness of both the food poverty and insecurity crisis, and the need for long-term solutions to its root causes. The extent to which such national and local organisations and campaigns can elicit *policy* change on welfare, tax and income, and living costs will become apparent over the coming years.

Nevertheless, hope and a sense of the possible is, arguably, more likely to be found within social and familial solidarities outside food aid organisations and high-profile food poverty coalitions. In the midst of destitution, family members, neighbours and friends may provide emotional, childcare and material support, as identified by my own research with white British and Pakistani food insecure women in Bradford. Among Pakistani women, in particular, the normality and regularity of sharing food between households, regardless of affluence, cemented the celebrated interdependency of the community. Relationships of exchange were based not on self-interest but pursued in the interest of the well-being of each individual, who together composed the community. Thus, oppositional movements and communal existence, based on solidarity and reciprocation and materialising in food redistribution, persist outside the more conspicuous forms of food charity typified by Trussell Trust food banks and high-profile campaigns. It is from these coexisting constructs of being, so divergent from neoliberal norms and behaviours, that we may find real hope and a sense of the possible.

As key components of a broad strategy to reduce food insecurity in the United Kingdom, three immediate actions could be:

1. Secure an exit from all UK food banks by 2030. In the short-term, this will require local government and key third-sector stakeholders to design and implement a food bank exit strategy, planning the actions needed to ensure that people in food insecurity have effective and immediate access to advice and cash-based entitlements during a financial crisis.
2. Further support and develop grassroots alliances tackling food poverty and insecurity at the local level. Encourage and assist alliances to engage local policymakers and politicians in solving the root causes of food insecurity; and support people with lived experience of food insecurity to take on governance roles.
3. Local authorities should fully implement the real Living Wage for all their direct employees and their service suppliers' workers, in line with accreditation as a Living Wage Employer. All local authorities should ensure that all who provide council services are paid at least the real Living Wage, including care workers, school staff and waste collection workers.

WHAT WILL IT TAKE TO END HUNGER IN THE UNITED KINGDOM?

Niall Cooper

Urban communities have long experience of poverty, but did any of us ever expect the re-emergence of hunger as a social reality in twenty-first century Britain? Food poverty is not an exclusively urban problem, but it certainly has had a severe impact on people in urban areas – and not just those 'traditionally' associated with high levels of poverty.

Emma's story of life in food poverty in Cambridge is typical of many:

> I am a single mum of three and have used food banks three times since November 2017. It felt really awful to be in that position; I went from a £30,000-a-year job in HR to ending up there in six months. Following my husband and I separating, he left me with a lot of debt and I couldn't sustain living costs and childcare on my own so I had to give up my job and claim income support.
>
> It's really hard to go to the food bank when you are used to doing your own shopping and supporting yourself. The volunteers were really good and didn't judge but I still got upset, and they were comforting. At the time, I hadn't realised you're limited to how many times you can use food banks per year and I found that concept quite bizarre. It's there to help people when they are in need but you can't dictate when and how many times they will be in need – everyone's circumstances are different.

Every story of food poverty is different, but every story is one story too many. Yet with up to eight million households experiencing some level of 'household food insecurity'[7] this is the painful truth for far too many people in urban communities.

As the Joseph Rowntree Foundation has painstakingly documented,[8] we are now living in a decade of destitution, of squeezed incomes, rising living costs, and households trapped with rising levels of debt and little or no savings to fall back on, and in many cases literally nothing left in the cupboard. This leaves families with little resilience against even the smallest shocks to their income.

Research by the Social Market Foundation[9] found that four in ten individuals with a household income of £10,000 or less, reported that groceries were a strain on finances. A quarter of individuals said that healthy and nutritious food was unaffordable in the United Kingdom. One in ten said that they had cut back on their own food consumption so that others in their family (such as children) could eat.

The Social Market Foundation suggests that about one in ten deprived areas in England and Wales are 'food deserts' – areas that are poorly served by food stores. In these areas, individuals without a car or with mobility difficulties may struggle to access a wide range of healthy, affordable food. Examples include the Marsh Farm estate in Luton, the Southampton Way estate in South London, the Trowbridge area of Cardiff and Swarcliffe in Leeds. In Scotland, estates such as Easterhouse in Glasgow were identified as food deserts. Up to 1.2 million individuals in deprived areas live in food deserts.

Food poverty in the United Kingdom is not fundamentally an issue of a shortage of food, but a shortage of income. This fact has been extensively researched and documented in recent years, including by the Fabian Commission on Food and Poverty in 2015, in various reports from the All Party Parliamentary Group on Food Poverty/Feeding Britain since 2015, and the Children's Future Food Inquiry which reported in April 2019.[10]

The good news is that literally thousands of local faith and community groups have stepped up to the plate in recent years, not only through the estimated two thousand food banks across the United Kingdom, but also through a huge array of other community food projects, community cafes, growing schemes, social supermarkets and the like. Delve into just about any urban community and you will find an array of formal and informal groups engaged in some form of food-related provision. On the one hand, this demonstrates the immense power of civil society, and the resilience and inventiveness of local communities, but on the other, it highlights the increasing inability (or unwillingness) of the state to ensure access to the basic necessities of life.

This paradox poses a key challenge for urban communities: how might it be possible to move away from the model of emergency food aid typified by the twenty-first-century foodbank, to more sustainable long-term solutions?

In the United States and Canada there was a similar move to establish food banks in response to an 'urgent crisis' facing communities more than three decades ago. Now, what was once considered 'emergency' provision has become institutionalised and corporatised. In contrast, the two main foodbank networks in the United Kingdom – the Trussell Trust and the Independent Food Aid Network – are working hard to develop strategies to put themselves out of business within the next ten years.

In the meantime, there is an urgent need for more coordinated and considered approaches. While much of the activity that has sprung up in urban communities in response to the growth of food poverty is heroic, it can also be uncoordinated, short term, constantly re-inventing the wheel – and failing to learn or share lessons from similar groups down the road, let alone the other side of the country.

The Food Power programme, run jointly by Sustain and Church Action on Poverty, is working with more than sixty-five local Food Poverty Alliances to try and address this problem, sharing good practice within and across towns and cities, promoting more 'upstream' approaches, encouraging community and voluntary groups to work more closely not just with each other, but with local welfare assistance schemes, Healthy Start and other public health initiatives, and to jointly develop coordinated 'Local Food Poverty Action Plans'.

A second key challenge is to ensure not only that people are fed, but that their dignity is protected and affirmed in the process.

In Scotland, the Dignity in Practice project[11] works alongside community food groups and organisations to explore what promoting and enhancing dignity looks like in community food provision. Its peer support programme encourages changes in practice to recognise the important role of community initiatives as sources of support to people experiencing food insecurity, as well as inclusive spaces for people to access, share and enjoy food, regardless of their circumstances.

Working with people who have first-hand experience of food poverty, the Dignity Project has identified five key 'dignity principles' for community food providers to consider in the design and delivery of their work. These include a sense of control, the ability to take part in community life, the ability to be nourished and supported, to be involved in decision-making and to be valued and able to contribute.

While some commentators argue that any projects using surplus food to feed people are inherently undignified, others have focused on the important community-building role that food can play. The act of sharing food is one of the most basic things we can do together as human beings.

Local Pantries are one of the most promising and replicable local responses that offer a sustainable and dignified alternative to emergency food aid. Local Pantries are member-run food clubs that enable people in urban neighbourhoods to access good quality food (including fresh fruit and veg, dairy, meat, frozen and children's food) while at the same time typically saving £15–20 on their weekly shopping bills. There are currently around a dozen members of the Your Local Pantry network, ranging from Aberdeen to Cardiff and London to Preston. A social impact report highlighted that the benefits of Local Pantry membership are 'more than just a full tummy', but also include improvements to health and well-being, reduced stress and social isolation and increased skills and employability.[12]

The last, and most important, challenge facing urban communities is that civil society alone can't solve the problem of food poverty and hunger. In the long term, charitable food aid 'solutions' to the problem of food poverty are neither feasible nor desirable. While the idea of a 'right to food' is contested in the United Kingdom, there is broad agreement that it is the duty of government to ensure the welfare of all its citizens. The evidence of recent years, however, as outlined by Madeleine Power in this chapter, is that the government's welfare reforms have made matters worse.

The End Hunger UK campaign – which brings together a broad range of people and organisations, including many of the main charities working on food poverty at national level – has a bold vision of a country in which everyone has access to good food and no one has to go to bed hungry.

End Hunger UK's core partners, including Trussell Trust and the Independent Food Aid Network, as well as Oxfam and Church Action on Poverty, are clear that in spite of the fantastic voluntary efforts of thousands of people donating to and volunteering at food banks or other community food projects, the scale of food poverty continues to increase.

The conclusion is simple: we can only realise our vision of a country free from hunger if the government also acts. Only central government has the power to mobilise the resources, policies and legislative power to end UK hunger. This does not mean that the government should act alone, but it must take the lead.

In signing up to the UN Sustainable Development Goals, the UK government has already made a commitment to achieving zero hunger in the United Kingdom by 2030, as unlike the previous Millennium Development Goals, the Sustainable Development Goals apply equally to 'developed' and 'developing' countries. But achieving this goal will require a clear road map, coordinating the efforts of multiple government departments, local government, the voluntary and charity sector and many others.

End Hunger UK is therefore calling on the UK government to publicly affirm its commitment to ending hunger in the United Kingdom by 2030, and to develop a concrete plan to halve the numbers of people in household food insecurity by 2025 as a stepping stone towards this goal. Most importantly, the plan will need to focus on tackling the underlying factors which sweep far too many households into household food insecurity in the first place.

Key areas for action include ensuring that children have access to good food through statutory funded programmes including free meals not just during term time, but also during long school holidays; ensuring households facing an unexpected cash crisis (whether as a result of the cooker breaking, family bereavement or other unexpected bills) are able to access crisis welfare support and cash payments, such as those provided through the Scottish Welfare Fund; and fixing Universal Credit and the benefits system to ensure that in future we all have access to an adequate welfare safety net that works when we need it most.

In the sixth-wealthiest country on the planet, that should not be too much to ask. The solutions exist, but sadly, the political will is currently lacking.

For all the coverage given to food banks in recent years, tackling hunger is not currently a key priority for government. In the past two years, as a result of sustained pressure from campaigners and a small but dedicated group of cross-party MPs, the government has been pushed into some modest steps forward. Since 2018, the Department for Education has funded pilot 'holiday food provision' programmes for up to 50,000 children in a limited number of areas; in the 2018 autumn budget the government was forced to inject £1.8 billion extra into fixing some of the worst problems associated with Universal Credit; and in February 2019, the Office of National Statistics agreed for the first time to systematically measure the numbers of people experiencing household food insecurity in the United Kingdom.

These are small steps, but far from a recognition that government has any overall responsibility to ensure no one needs to go to bed hungry in the United Kingdom. As recently as June 2019, the government rejected the main findings of a Parliamentary inquiry into hunger, malnutrition and food insecurity, which revealed that no government department currently takes any responsibility for ensuring no one in the United Kingdom goes hungry, and called for the creation of a Minister for Hunger.[13]

Equally, it's important not to let opposition parties off the hook. For years the opposition has used 'food banks' as a proxy for attacking austerity but have failed to devise policies to explicitly address the issue of food poverty and hunger.

Given the failure of political leadership, it's up to us. Our task is to build the public and political will necessary to persuade the UK government (of whatever political persuasion) to step up to the plate. Tens of thousands of people work to address the effects of food poverty in communities across the United Kingdom every week. Our challenge is to turn even a fraction of this energy towards the goal of political change. Foodbank volunteers and users need to beat a path to the doors of their MPs to make the case for change.

Here are three actions that can be taken now to end food poverty:

1. Affirm the dignity of all who use any form of food charity. Treating those who have to rely on food aid as equals and partners, rather than victims, is the first step towards recognising that we cannot end food poverty without the creativity, engagement and ideas of those directly affected.
2. Look to shift the focus of local provision away from emergency food aid and towards approaches which provide potentially more sustainable and long-term ways of addressing the underlying drivers of poverty.

3. Government should develop a coordinated cross-departmental plan, involving a range of stakeholders (and crucially, people struggling against food poverty themselves) to ensure that everyone has access to good food and no one needs to go to bed hungry, with a clear target of halving household food insecurity by 2025 and a goal of zero hunger in the United Kingdom within ten years.

Together we can end hunger in the United Kingdom. Let's make sure we do.

Notes

1. Trussell Trust, 'Record 1.6m Food Bank Parcels Given to People in Past Year as the Trussell Trust Calls for End to Universal Credit Five Week Wait'. *Trussell Trust*, 2019. Accessed 7 April 2020. https://www.trusselltrust.org/2019/04/25/record-1-6m-food-bank-parcels/.
2. FAO, IFAD, WFP and WHO, 'The State of Food Insecurity and Nutrition in the World 2017'. FAO, 2017. Accessed 7 April 2020. http://www.fao.org/3/a-i7695e.pdf.
3. Food Standards Agency, 'The "Food and You" Survey Wave 4 (2016)' in the *"Food and You" Survey*', pp. 1–87 (London, Food Standards Agency, 2017).
4. House of Commons Environmental Audit Committee, '*Sustainable Development Goals in the UK Follow Up: Hunger, Malnutrition and Food Insecurity in the UK*'. House of Commons Environmental Audit Committee, 2019. Accessed 7 April 2020. https://publications.parliament.uk/pa/cm201719/cmselect/cmenvaud/1491/1491.pdf.
5. N. Amin Smith, D. Phillips and P. Simpson, 'Real-Terms Change in Local Government Service Spending by LA Decile of Grant Dependence, 2009–10 to 2016–17, England, Scotland and Wales'. London: Institute for Fiscal Studies, 2016.
6. Ibid.
7. 'Household Food Insecurity in the UK'. *ENUF*. Accessed 24 October 2019. https://enuf.org.uk/household-food-insecurity-uk.
8. S. Fitzpatrick et al., '*Destitution in the UK 2018*'. Joseph Rowntree Foundation, 2018. Accessed 7 April 2020. https://www.jrf.org.uk/report/destitution-uk-2018.
9. S. Corfe, '*What Are the Barriers to Eating Healthily in the UK?*'. Social Market Foundation, 2018. Accessed 7 April 2020. http://www.smf.co.uk/publications/barriers-eating-healthily-uk/.
10. 'The Children's Future Food Inquiry'. *The Food Foundation*. Accessed 24 October 2019. https://foodfoundation.org.uk/childrens-future-food-inquiry/.
11. 'Dignity in Practice' Project. *Nourish Scotland*. Accessed 24 October 2019. http://www.nourishscotland.org/projects/dignity/.
12. 'Your Local Pantry'. *Church Action on Poverty*. Accessed 24 October 2019. https://www.church-poverty.org.uk/what-we-do/pantry/.
13. 'Government Must Go Further to Tackle Hunger in UK'. Environmental Audit Committee, 26 June 2019. Accessed 7 April 2020. https://www.parliament.uk/business/committees/committees-a-z/commons-select/environmental-audit-committee/news-parliament-2017/sustainable-development-goals-government-response-published-17-19/.

Chapter 3

THE UNHOMED CITY

HOUSING CRISIS, AUSTERITY AND THE PRODUCTION OF PRECARIOUS LIVES

Emma Bimpson and Richard Goulding

Arguably the predominant diagnosis of the housing crisis is that it is a problem rooted in the insufficient supply of homes in relation to demand. With too few homes for too many people, the solution is for governments to help unlock the market, helping people to buy homes and encouraging developers to build more. Implicitly, this treats housing as a commodity like any other privately consumed good. Here perhaps the key aspirational group, to which policy should respond, is the homeowner. Yet the home is more than a commodity among many others that we may choose to consume. Given its critical role as shelter and a dwelling it is an essential prerequisite, and the very basis, of the collective means through which our lives are produced.

If we are to adequately grasp something we can call the housing crisis, we must look beyond supply and demand to the key power relations that shape our cities and homes as well as to forms of inequality focused around the varying precarity of paid and unpaid labour today. This becomes particularly clear when we explore what happens when housing and the land it sits on is treated as a tradeable good like any other. Generating a profit from urban development is a risky endeavour, requiring capital to be tied up for long periods of time in spatially fixed real estate, exposed to the vagaries of market forces. To overcome these risks, real estate needs finance to provide access to capital, enabling the built environment to act as a profitable outlet for investment for banks, institutional investors and other financial institutions seeking a strong return. The scarcity of land means this is a process easily speculated on. This in turn means that homes can be bought and sold solely in order to make a profit, rather than recognising the core role of homes as social assets. Speculation in housing markets takes many forms, but the risks of this process and inequalities within cities makes this a crisis-prone process, intensifying the divide between social groups, causing gentrification, the creation and destruction of homes, as well as potentially volatile property bubbles whose collapse can suddenly destroy the value of homes and lead poorer owners to lose their homes.

While speculation has been common throughout the process of urbanisation, the intensified volatility of housing bubbles in countries such as the United Kingdom since the social and economic crises of the 1970s has led an increasing number of commentators to argue that land and housing is undergoing what is called 'financialisation'. This term refers to the increased accumulation of profits through financial mechanisms, rather than the production and trade of goods and services.[1] Housing has been at the forefront of this process, as protective barriers between mortgage and capital markets designed to prevent the use of homes in speculative investment were taken down in the 1980s. This enabled housing to be treated as an investment asset by financial institutions, including the sale of mortgage debt owned by banks as a new form of investment in its own right. This process was by securitisation in which mortgages, rents and other income streams could be repackaged and sold on as bonds, and vehicles such as Real Estate Investment Trusts, publicly listed companies that enabled investors to trade in shares of property without having a vested interest in the underlying assets beyond the rents they can yield. These changes helped cement the role of housing as tradeable asset, diminishing its role as a core element of social life.

Allowing investors to enter real estate markets without having to gain in-depth knowledge of local conditions has enabled a flood of capital into housing since the 1990s, inflating land values and amplifying speculative property cycles in multiple countries and cities, shaped by local and institutional contexts. The triggering of the 2007–2009 financial crisis by the collapse of speculative trades in so-called sub-prime mortgages revealed how these seemingly abstract flows of money are rooted in the physical urban landscape. While the crash caused initial capital flight from securitised residential mortgage markets, the links between financial speculation and the urban landscape have nonetheless been rebuilt over the past ten years.

One example of financialisation in motion can be seen in cities like Manchester which has, since the 1990s, pursued a model of property-led regeneration, focusing on attracting private real estate investment to renew its economy through means such as developer-friendly planning measures, set-piece regeneration projects such as the 2002 Commonwealth Games and the selective demolition of some inner-city neighbourhoods. The city has succeeded in bringing people back to its central core, resulting in a belt of new apartments running from Salford Quays in the west to the fringes of its city centre in the east and south. In the past decade its city council has entered into joint ventures with private investors to rebuild neighbourhoods on the edge of its city centre, such as the Abu Dhabi United Group through its Manchester Life development company in Ancoats, and the Northern Gateway in Collyhurst with Hong Kong developers Far East Consortium. These often opaque multimillion-pound deals and their production of expensive city centre flats sit alongside a growing crisis in street and invisible homelessness and an ongoing lack of affordable housing, raising uncomfortable questions about who the city is for.[2]

A key enabler of financialisation has been the central government-led erosion of public housing, allowing urban land to be re-commodified and unlocked for investment. A major form this has taken in the United Kingdom has been through the Right to Buy (RTB) since the 1980s, enabling existing tenants of local government-owned 'council' housing to buy their homes at a generous discount, while preventing replacements from being built. With what has come to be known as social housing now being delivered primarily by non-state providers such as housing associations, the sector has been residualised as, increasingly, poorer households are left in the sector. Meanwhile, chronic shortfalls in affordable housing and the rising expense of home ownership are leading the private rented sector (PRS) to return as a mainstream tenure. In Manchester, this has been exacerbated by a reluctance by its local government to pressure developers to make affordable housing contributions, prioritising instead the increase of private supply for people who can afford to live in the city centre.

The costs of central and local government approaches are now reaching crisis point. Worse, government action to reduce government deficits in the aftermath of the state-backed bank bailouts of 2008 has led to massive public cuts over ten years of austerity. Since the election of David Cameron's Conservative-led government (2010–16), funds for traditional social housing have been cut almost completely. What remaining grants there are have been switched to market-focused intermediate tenures such as shared ownership, half owned and half rented by social housing tenants, and 'Affordable Rent', at up to 80 per cent of market rate. Deep welfare cuts have disproportionately impacted groups including low income, young and disabled people, while the use of punitive sanctions in welfare payments has significantly increased. Housing benefit, a means-tested social security payment for living costs, has also been made less secure, including through the 'Bedroom Tax', a reduction in benefit for people in social housing deemed to have one or more spare rooms, and the Benefit Cap, which limits the total amount a household can receive in benefits. Universal Credit, paid five weeks in arrears directly to claimants rather than landlords, has increased the risk of arrears for people on low incomes. Local housing allowance (LHA) caps in the PRS have also restricted the benefits available to people renting privately, while people aged 35 and under are limited to shared accommodation. These financial and austerity-driven factors have brought dramatic consequences for people looking for a home within our cities.

The precarity that exists in our heavily investment-focused cities is perhaps most visible in rising numbers of homeless people sleeping rough, who depend upon public spaces, local authority housing services, day centres, night shelters, and increasingly, hospital accident and emergency departments for shelter and support. In major cities such as London, Manchester and Birmingham, rough sleeping has risen substantially since 2010,[3] including people from European Economic Area (EEA) countries who have been denied housing benefit since 2014. Yet official rough sleeper counts have received criticism for understating the problem, where outreach activity is focused on 'known places'. On entering cities like Manchester by train it is possible to see tents tucked away in the corners of urban green space and wasteland, while others find even more hidden places to shelter.

Legislation, including the archaic 1824 Vagrancy Act, and Public Space Protection Orders (PSPOs), policing and private security have operated to disperse and criminalise tent dwelling and begging that is perceived to intimidate or pose health risks to the public. Yet many argue that these unaccountable civil enforcement measures merely serve to reinforce poverty and marginalisation by imposing financial penalties on individuals who are already unable to pay. The criminal justice system is also implicated in creating more disorderly means of survival, with reports suggesting that 50 per cent of women leaving HMP Bronzefield in Surrey, the largest female prison in Europe, are released with no means of accessing accommodation, some leaving with tents. For both men and women leaving custody, access to housing as well as basic welfare provisions more generally, remains an urgent need.

With chronic social housing shortages, private landlords increasingly operate as an arm of the welfare state. People who are not considered to be in priority need, or who are found to be 'intentionally homeless' by local authorities for reasons such as criminal convictions or rent arrears, are limited to hostels, privately owned hotels, bed and breakfast accommodation, and short-term private rented accommodation. Research and campaigning organisations have exposed a steep rise in emergency and temporary housing options for people who have become homeless and the inadequacies of those provisions, even with recently extended duties under the Homelessness Reduction Act in England in 2018. While private providers capitalise on the housing benefit payments they receive from local authorities, some of the poorest housing has been found in unsupported temporary accommodation, where drug use, violence and unsanitary conditions are often common. Among the worst outcomes are the conditions of people seeking refuge and asylum, despite multimillion-pound contracts being awarded to those companies ostensibly in charge of looking after their housing and well-being.

The risks of dependency on private housing markets are further exposed as the ending of a PRS tenancy remains one of the biggest causes of homelessness.

While local authorities increasingly rely on PRS accommodation to meet their housing duties, access to private tenancies is dependent on the goodwill of landlords who have found themselves at the centre of homeless prevention strategies. When 94 per cent of privately rented homes have been found to be unaffordable to people receiving housing benefit, the supply and demand narrative of housing crisis becomes even more untenable.[4] The commodification of housing and the privatisation of urban space is not only a feature of new 'luxury' apartment blocks on the horizon; it stretches across society.

The barriers to housing presented by markets and restricted welfare subsidy not only impact people in the most immediate housing need, but also limit housing options and tenancy security for renters more broadly. In response to these conditions growing numbers of renters' unions, campaigns and policy debates have acknowledged the precarity presented by what many now see as a state-sponsored expansion in private landlordism, not least through the flow of billions to landlords in housing benefit. However, the value of housing as a place where social stability can be produced and maintained has also been undermined in the social rented sector. Both housing associations and councils have increased the stringency of pre-tenancy assessments to exclude likely 'tenancy failures', including people with previous debt, rent arrears and inability to pay rent in advance, which mirrors commercial practices and impacts young people in particular.[5]

These changes do not mean that the use of urban space and houses as commodities is inevitable. The unequal and problematic terrain created by financialisation is also the space within which uses of the city are increasingly contested. Both the United Kingdom and Ireland in the past five years have seen the rise of tenant unions fighting to organise renters, including groups such as Glasgow Living Rent, the London Renters Union, Community and Tenants' Action in Dublin and Acorn in cities including Manchester, Brighton, Bristol and Newcastle. While their overall numbers are still small, these organisations demonstrate one form in which people are building solidarity against the individualised precariousness of the housing crisis.

In addition to these oppositional movements, the spread of community land trusts into urban areas over the past decade has acted as a vehicle for residents to directly take over stewardship of their neighbourhoods in projects such as Granby 4 Streets and Homebaked in central Liverpool, which have experienced decades of demolition and state-led gentrification. Community land trusts, originating in the civil rights movement of the United States in the 1960s, also spread to the United Kingdom in the 2000s, placing ownership of land into a not-for-profit trust for communal benefit. Another important example of positive change can be seen in self-help housing, used in cities such as Leeds, where homeless and other volunteers bring empty housing back into use. While community groups with limited cash resources, operating in land markets dominated by private property relations, should not be expected to act as a substitute for badly needed public investment, they act as a space for experiments in collective living that inform alternative forms of cities that we may wish to create.

Finally, some local authorities and housing associations within the social housing sector are trialling new forms of homelessness support. Alongside housing associations and other not-for-profit groups attempting to circumvent the private market by establishing social lettings agencies, some cities have embarked on large-scale 'Housing First' pilots that involve several social landlords in providing accommodation for rough sleepers, and people experiencing poor mental health and addiction. However, as many pilots have demonstrated, the unconditional offer of housing, as well as the availability of flexible and intensive wrap-around support, remain substantial barriers given the complexity of need among the people these projects aim to help. Further funding to continue Housing First after pilots end is uncertain, another demonstration of the self-defeating limits that austerity generates.

The above issues demonstrate that solving the housing crisis must look beyond supply and demand. These problems are long-term, structural and complex. But they are also political, and dependent on the relationships that individuals have with powers and authorities that govern struggles in the urban landscape. Solving the housing crisis ultimately requires finding alternatives to the speculative model of housing development which dominates our cities, increasingly colonised by high finance. Properly resourced public housing and rent controls are needed to bring down over-inflated land markets. In the shorter term, this must also include immediate measures to rebuild the safety net of the welfare state, such as reversing housing benefit and other welfare cuts. The private actors used to deliver temporary and emergency accommodation must be made accountable through properly resourced regulation by central and local government. For solutions to be successful, however, they must go beyond technical fixes and look to build on forms of goodwill and collective solidarity now evident in many of our towns and cities.

In the short term, here are three immediate steps we should take:

1. Develop a more effective regulatory regime for private landlords and empower councils to take private rented housing that fails these standards into public ownership.
2. Remove the Local Housing Allowance cap for people living in private rented housing, which will not only ensure that the benefit adequately covers rent but will prevent discrimination by private landlords against people receiving LHA.
3. Provide local authorities with adequate funding to provide independent housing and necessary social support through Housing First and similarly successful local programmes.

COUNCIL HOUSING IN THE URBAN MIXER

Glyn Robbins

The Current Crisis

We seem increasingly incapable of finding a decent home for a significant proportion of our population. The number of households in substandard, unaffordable and insecure housing is rising – to the point at which such problems now appear normal or everyday conditions without resolution. These issues are also feeding the growth of homelessness and the deepening of a range of social and personal problems associated with a failing system for meeting what the United Nations regards as 'the right to live somewhere in security, peace and dignity'.[6] Whether this situation constitutes a 'crisis' is sometimes the subject of academic discussion. Some argue what we're seeing is just the normal workings of our growth-oriented economy.[7] Those debates can appear disconnected from the urgent needs of millions whose lives are blighted by chronic policy failure.

Over the course of nearly half a century, governments of all stripes have reduced housing rights and entitlements, particularly as council housing has been eroded. Policymakers and the general populace appear to have become ever more deeply obsessed with private property and a kind of deification of houses as the means of making money, rather than homes. Home ownership dominates policy interventions, to the exclusion of alternatives. Today private landlords that have bought homes to seek personal profit are given enormous windfalls via state benefits.[8] Alongside these shifts, the proven ability of council housing to offer affordable and decent accommodation to those on low incomes has been under sustained attack, as part of a wider dismantling of the welfare state and post-war settlement. The winners in this system have gained even more while the majority struggle or are stressed by their housing condition.

The Effects on People and Cities

A welter of statistics and reports illustrate the scale and impact of the housing crisis. At least 320,000 people in Britain are legally defined as homeless. Many more are in temporary, insecure, unaffordable, substandard or unsuitable accommodation.[9] The knock-on effects for the wider economy and society are massive. For example, according to the Office for Budget Responsibility (OBR), Housing Benefit cost £21.9 billion in 2017–18.[10] In 2011, the Building Research Establishment (BRE) estimated the cost to the NHS of poor housing at £1.4 billion a year.[11] In its most scandalous form we can now find 210,000 children registered as homeless, some of them living in shipping containers.[12] Meanwhile, the Office of National Statistics has estimated that 597 people died in 2017 as a direct or indirect result of being homeless, an increase of 24 per cent over the previous five years.[13]

There is a tendency to see the housing crisis as confined to London and the South-East, but it is national. Today 79 per cent of households on council waiting lists are outside the capital, nearly one-third in shire districts.[14] Rents in the private sector, in which 20 per cent of the population are housed, have increased significantly all over the country since 2015,[15] as has the gap between earnings and house prices.[16]

These issues impact on people's daily lives, but are part of a wider context of urban malaise. Cities across the planet have been subject to a fundamental reordering of urban space. Globally property is now valued at $226 trillion, of which housing constitutes 75 per cent. High-rise apartment blocks, often with accompanying high-end shops, gyms and restaurants have become a ubiquitous feature of many of our city and townscapes. Areas where working-class communities once lived and worked have been transformed beyond recognition, leading to physical, economic and cultural displacement. The acquisition of land for speculative private property development, particularly in inner-urban areas the industry regards as 'high value', is a direct threat to the homes and services of the working-class people who live there. In the words of John Arena, these people are seen as 'an obstacle to the full spatial, cultural, political and economic emergence and maintenance of the neoliberal city, which can only be achieved by clearing the ground of poor people'.[17]

Many of these forces converge and collide at the Fox Gardens council estate in Islington, just outside the financial district of the City of London, where I've worked since 2011. It was built on vacant bomb sites in the mid-1960s by the newly created Greater London Council (GLC), a development that embodied post-war optimism. Many of the first tenants, some of whom still live there, were rehoused from the slums depicted in the TV documentary *Cathy Come Home* at around the same time. Their new environment was designed with the future in mind: flats and maisonettes of different sizes, some specifically for older people, others for single people and young families, with communal gardens, drying rooms and play areas. Norms of neighbourly behaviour and a sense of community identity took root in this new estate, some of which still endure. There is an active resident organisation and a genuine sense that people are looking out for each other.

Today, the working-class culture and social fabric of Fox Gardens are at risk. A relentless development frenzy, attracted to an area being rebranded as Tech City or 'Silicon Roundabout', surrounds the estate. Noise, traffic, pollution and disruption from building sites are constant. The consequences for people's mental and physical health are difficult to evaluate, but in my work around the estate I will regularly hear about stress-related illness, tensions between neighbours and plans to move away under the weight of development pressure and changes in the wider neighbourhood. What was once a settled, multigenerational community now experiences a turnover of around one-third of its residents every year.

The churning social context of the estate is emblematic of wider forces that have swept council housing within the property speculation economy. The impact of RTB is much lamented, well-chronicled, but often underestimated. Each sale reduces the stock of genuinely affordable rented homes and has multiple knock-on effects. The opportunity to buy a small bedsit at Fox Gardens, with a £100,000 discount, and then rent it out for £1,300 a month, or sell it for £300,000 can be too good to miss. A three-bedroom maisonette costs a Fox Gardens council tenant about £600 a month, but is also capable of commanding a rent in the private market of £2,500 a month, or a sale price of at least £700,000.

With such economic incentives, it's no surprise that the next RTB sale at Fox Gardens will make council tenants on the estate a minority. About half the homes sold are now lived in by private renters, most of them young housesharers. Many pass through like ships in the night. They are part of the exponential rise in private renting that is the direct and intended corollary to four decades of attacks on council housing.

The normalising of exorbitant rents and perennial insecurity for private tenants contributes to a wider sense of instability and insecurity on the estate. Fox Gardens has long had a high degree of social and ethnic diversity, with numerous mother tongues and residents who range from professors to street cleaners. The image of council housing as a monoculture has never been true, but it's an unintended consequence of council house sales that it has brought people to live on estates who might not have otherwise. But the overheated housing market is changing that. Living at Fox Gardens is now too expensive for many, particularly with restrictions on Housing Benefit. New private tenants are coming from a narrower social base, shifting the demographic. New council tenants are few and far between, but tend to have more complex needs as tenancies are increasingly granted to those in the most desperate circumstances.

For existing residents these changes have contributed to a sense that the place they call home is slipping away. Change is constant. Familiar shops, pubs and market stalls have been replaced with those catering to a more affluent clientele. In an area that once had a lot of small manufacturing industries, one of the biggest new property developments is called the White Collar Factory, apparently without irony. Immediately opposite the estate, a swanky new office is due to be occupied by CNN, bringing the prospect of a 1,000-strong, 24/7, high-paid professional workforce. Caught in the vortex is a generation of young, working-class people whose profound sense of dispossession shows itself in depressingly regular incidents of sometimes deadly violence.

If these trends – and the government policies that encourage them – continue, it is likely that Fox Gardens won't be a council estate in 10 years' time. Across the United Kingdom and especially in London, council estates are under threat from a toxic cocktail of budget cuts, predatory capital and compliant councils. The long thread of hostility towards municipal housing is reaching an endgame in which the fundamental question is whether the land under the homes of thousands should be sold to realise its market value. Ted Turner, the boss of CNN, could come to their London office one day, look out of the window towards Fox Gardens and see a golden commercial opportunity.

A Sense of the Possible

Fox Gardens residents will fight to defend their homes and take action to ensure they aren't the passive victims of social engineering and urban colonialism. They're organised as a Tenant Management Organisation (TMO), a kind of body that has a complex role, made more so by the fallout from the Grenfell Tower atrocity. TMOs can be seen as part of a privatisation agenda and they certainly encourage parochialism. However, they also provide a legally constituted forum through which people living on council estates can take meaningful, collective decisions. These can include important operational management issues, as well as organising community activities, but they can extend to more fundamental challenges to establishment power structures. For example, Fox Gardens TMO has repeatedly taken up the cause of residents suffering disturbance from inconsiderate contractors in the area and has compelled them to restrict their activities and be mindful of the fact that their work site is also someone's home.

The TMO is also contesting the plans of Islington Council to redevelop Fox Gardens. In doing so, they are asserting their rights as residents and defying some deep-rooted institutional practices. In 2015, the Council announced its intention to build 30–40 new homes on the estate, most of them by adding an extra layer on top of Fox Gardens. This was met with immediate resistance. Although the TMO recognised and supported the need to build new homes, particularly council housing, there was scepticism about how it was going to be done and more generally, a feeling that residents had just had enough of living in the midst of building sites. The Council's response was to point to the 18,000 families on its housing waiting list, a form of emotional blackmail reinforced by suggestions that estate residents would get 'first dibs' on the new homes. Using the standard procedure, the Council sought to engage residents in a 'consultation' process. But this met with limited success when it became apparent, over the course of four years, that none of the residents' suggestions were being listened to or taken seriously.

The Council's plans remained virtually unchanged from their original form, despite the TMO raising numerous questions and objections. So in May 2019, the TMO decided to get a second opinion by appointing its own architects to explore the feasibility of building the new homes, but minimising the impact on existing residents. By taking back some control over the development process and refusing to be the subjects of the Council's agenda, Fox Gardens' residents were acting in the best tradition of independent tenant organisations and asserting not just their legal right to manage, but their right simply to retain a foothold in the city they currently live in.

TMOs aren't a panacea, but neither are they a placebo. They demonstrate the potential for people to take control of their homes and environment, provided they're not constituted in the perverted form that existed in Kensington and Chelsea before Grenfell. For example, in recent years, Fox Gardens TMO has retained a dedicated estate handyperson, dumped a contractor who refused to pay the London Living Wage, introduced a programme of small improvements to tenants' homes, supported local arts and drama projects, won awards for its communal gardens and launched an estate 'upcycling' project. Perhaps above all, it has provided a housing service with a human face. Along with other Islington TMOs, Fox Gardens was also an early part of the successful grassroots movement that rose up against the 2016 Housing and Planning Act which threatened to fatally wound council housing.

An Agenda for Change

The key national policy changes and their lived experience in estates like Fox Gardens are critical to the future of British cities. The forces swirling around Fox Gardens are part of bigger processes now threatening to dislocate many working-class urban communities, for which council housing has been the bedrock. The universally acknowledged housing crisis has produced a growing rhetorical consensus that there is a need for a restoration of council housing to the policy mainstream, but how, or if, this will be achieved is less clear. The government has said it will lift borrowing restrictions on councils wanting to build. This would help in some areas, but not in those that misguidedly transferred their council homes to private housing associations. In opposition, the Labour Party has signalled a more radical approach, but without any firm commitment to council housing. This equivocal policy is already being implemented in London where Mayor Sadiq Khan has loudly announced a commitment to build 11,000 new council homes. But there is emerging evidence that these will be at significantly higher rents, creating a two-tier system and undermining the only genuinely affordable rented housing in places where the market is pricing people out of their communities.

Fox Gardens offers a more realistic and sustainable model for urban hope. The power and agency that comes from independent tenant and resident organisations doesn't have to take the form of a TMO, but similar forms of social organisation will be essential for rebuilding the kind of civic engagement that may otherwise be lost in the neoliberal onslaught. Such organisations can build social unity in defiance of the individualism the market system encourages while raising the quality of services and conditions in the neighbourhood. Asserting the principle that housing should be a social asset, not a private commodity, is intrinsic to council housing and has vital importance if we are to seriously address climate change. The potential for services to be shared and locally based is demonstrated by council housing, but can extend beyond it. As generations of council tenants can testify, having a home that's secure, truly affordable, well maintained and not subject to the whims of the market helps its residents to control their housing, instead of being controlled by it.

Now is the time to develop a new agenda for council housing, based on its tried and tested qualities, but linking them to a wider vision for the type of society we want to live in. Critical issues around land, natural resources, health, social care and well-being can all be addressed through campaigns for a housing system that isn't predicated on private profit. To achieve this, in January 2019, the Homes for All alliance (which grew out of the campaign against the Housing and Planning Act) produced a Charter for Housing Action, calling for a 20-year programme to build 3.1 million homes for social rent, including 100,000 new council homes a year, more effective regulation of all landlords, a revival of independent tenant organisations and reform of private renting, including rent control and scrapping of 'no-fault' evictions. During the year, these demands entered the mainstream. In late July 2019, Channel 4 aired *George Clarke's Council House Scandal*, after which an online petition calling for 100,000 council homes a year was signed by 210,000 people. On 24 September, the Labour Party's annual conference unanimously passed a resolution backing the same call and went further by calling for the scrapping of RTB.

After decades of retreat in the face of the neoliberal onslaught, the housing agenda is shifting, in the direction of fulfilling the UN's mission for everyone to have the right to live somewhere in security, peace and dignity.

Distilling the above into three immediate priorities, we should:

1. Undertake concerted public investment in housing. Instead of spending billions on helping existing homebuyers or on Housing Benefit, a significant switch should be made to commit to a 20-year programme to build 3.1 million homes for social rent, including 100,000 new council homes a year.
2. Reform private renting by introducing rent control and scrapping 'no-fault' evictions.
3. Provide funding to help a revival of independent tenant organisations to improve community participation and cohesion.

Notes

1. R. Rolnik, *Urban Warfare: Housing under the Empire of Finance* (London: Verso, 2019).
2. R. Goulding and J. Silver, 'From Homes to Assets. Housing Financialisation in Manchester'. Update for financial year 2018/19. Greater Manchester Housing Action, 2019. Accessed 16 April 2020. http://www.gmhousingaction.com/from-homes-to-assets-an-update-on-housing-financialisation-in-manchester-for-2018-19/.
3. S. Fitzpatrick et al., *The Homelessness Monitor: England 2019* (London: Crisis, 2019).
4. 'Locked Out: How Britain Keeps People Homeless'. Bureau of Investigative Journalism, 4 October 2019. Accessed 16 April 2020. https://www.thebureauinvestigates.com/stories/2019-10-04/locked-out-how-britain-keeps-people-homeless.
5. J. Preece and E. Bimpson, *Forms and Mechanisms of Exclusion in Contemporary Housing Systems – An Evidence Review*. 2019. Accessed 16 April 2020. https://housingevidence.ac.uk/wp-content/uploads/2019/04/1904-Mechanisms-of-exclusion-evidence-review_final.pdf.
6. Office of the United Nations High Commissioner for Human Rights, *The Right to Adequate Housing* (Geneva: UNHCR, 2014).
7. See, for example, D. Madden and P. Marcuse. *In Defense of Housing* (London: Verso, 2016).
8. S. Wilcox and P. Williams, *Dreams and Reality? Government Finance, Taxation and the Private Housing Market* (Coventry: Chartered Institute of Housing, 2018).
9. P. Butler, *At least 320,000 Homeless People in Britain, Shelter Say*, Guardian, 22 November 2018.
10. Office for Budget Responsibility (OBR), *Welfare Spending: Housing Benefit*, 15 May 2018. Accessed 16 April 2020. https://obr.uk/forecasts-in-depth/tax-by-tax-spend-by-spend/welfare-spending-housing-benefit/.
11. Building Research Establishment (BRE), *The Cost of Poor Housing to the NHS*, Briefing Paper (Bracknell: BRE, 2011).
12. Children's Commissioner, *Bleak Houses: Tackling the Crisis of Family Homelessness in England*, August 2019.
13. Office of National Statistics (ONS), *Deaths of Homeless People in England and Wales: 2013–2017*, 20 December 2018 (London: ONS, 2018).
14. Ministry of Housing, Communities and Local Government (MHCLG), *Households on LA Waiting Lists*, Live Table 600 (London: MHCLG, 2018).

15 House of Commons Library, *Private Rented Housing: The Rent Control Debate*, Briefing Paper no. 6760, 2019.
16 Office for National Statistics, *Housing Affordability Worsening in All LA Areas (England and Wales)* (London: ONS, 2018).
17 J. Arena, *Driven from New Orleans: How Nonprofits Betray Public Housing and Promote Privatization*, p. xxi (Minneapolis: University of Minnesota Press, 2012).

Chapter 4

THE ANXIOUS CITY

REDISCOVERING 'WE-NESS'

Rhiannon Corcoran

Fret in Urbe

My unit.
My lonely house.
Surrounded by others' hutches,
Connected to no lives.

The capital of capitals has been traded.
This place of red lines and prime sites
Exists only as planned opportunities, supporting little futures,
Neither called nor yearned for. Not heart-felt.

Cul-de-sacs of angst bleed across this map.
Stress Way, Dormitory Fields, Blue Pastures
Backdrops for individuals,
On a stage un-set for fuller, richer, cherished lives.

Yet, I remember …
Lettuces and onions grown in own, black yard earth.
Shared over ferny walls across acres of streets,
Enjoyed at bread and cheese teatimes set on damask tables,
Then re-enjoyed, caterpillars n' all, in comfy conversation on neighbouring steps.

When we had so little.
When we had so much.

In this chapter I argue that urban stress can be understood when we consider the central importance of three interrelated factors:

- The demise of social capital within the context of a dominant economic political philosophy,
- The critical importance that places play in supporting community wellbeing and the failure of modern places in this regard,
- The importance of addressing the effects of twenty-first-century urban living on young people.

Addressing and understanding these issues in future urban policy will address urban distress and provide an agenda of urban hope.

Social capital is the climax of humanity and among the most important features of successful human habitats. We need social support, we find joy in social relationships and we use social cognition. Our feeling for others is what makes both culture and compassionate society. Our ability and need to cooperate in joint ventures, even in the context of competition, is, as far as we can tell, unrivalled across the animal kingdom.

The social pinnacle we have reached has been accomplished through our ability to contemplate the lives of others and then to communicate those contemplations to others through language so that we act on them together in ways that demonstrate the importance of 'we-ness' to us. We are an altruistic species, yet society has fallen away from our lives. Places that support community are as rarefied now as a living museum. To know and to trust one's neighbour whose discretion can be counted on because our collective concerns exist beyond tittle-tattle and gossip is no longer commonplace. Without others we are isolated, we suffer and we age too young. Social and emotional loneliness are sources of deep distress, associated both with physical ill-health and with the common mental health difficulties of depression and anxiety.

Why then do we not properly consider people and their needs for community when we govern, plan and construct our places? The *entitativity*,[1] or sense of a meaningful whole, of the contemporary urban spaces that make up our habitats exists only on plans as blocks, quarters, sectors and units. It does not exist as social networks, neighbourliness, trust and friendly nods from locally rooted business folk who know, by knowing us, what we need and want. Such regeneration sites cannot support social capital because no consideration has been given to it. In this process, existing places are dismembered by highways, given purposefully functional names like the *Northern Distributor Road*. These 'opportunity sites' can become only isolated islands of development. Indeed, should they ever support successful gathering places, ingested pollution would become more of a worry. Recent evidence asserts the presence of particulates in probably every organ of our urban bodies. These inflammatory invaders, 'silent killers' according the World Health Organisation, are what makes air pollution a public health emergency (as Bethany Thompson's contribution in Chapter 6 discusses), dramatically affecting not only our physical but also our mental health.

It seems we've been doing nothing that is much good for us for decades.

In short, urbanism needs a new narrative.[2] Building the empathy back into planning, a discipline that emerged out of nineteenth-century public health concerns, is critically important. We can no longer afford to treat and gauge the success of our towns and cities primarily as engines to support economy, which disempower and disappoint swathes of us who need places to support our social existence. The new narrative must start and end with fulfilment and thriving. It should talk of lives well-lived and enjoyed, of places of meaning and purpose and it should embrace the sociability and pro-sociality of humanity and not just its productivity. This new narrative would make good economic sense too because the sustainable truth is that collective well-being, achieved via social capital, supports improved health and by doing so, makes for a thriving economy.

My opening poem suggests that we do know of ways to live in dense residential places that can boost society and neighbourliness, not invariably, but much more probably. If built environment professions prioritise people and social capital, this can play an important part in tempering and preventing future mental distress in our communities. Such re-thinking will re-establish a human habitat, supporting community within a reawakened practice of living environment.

What resources we have, what we regard as resources and how we treat those resources all need to be considered as we re-plan our habitats. Urban disadvantage is a long-standing, deliberate, debilitating set of circumstances. It encapsulates inequality in all its forms and provides the breeding ground for trauma, depression and anxiety. Evidence on the so-called urbanicity effect (the increased prevalence of mental distress in inner cities compared to more rural areas) robustly shows that these environments are toxic for children, leading to increased chance of both serious and common mental distress in adolescent and adult lives.

Never having enough and never being able to rely on the future delivering for you is a recipe for an unfulfilled and failing life. However, although poverty is hostile and disfavours cooperation, it does not always prevent strong community, just as wealth and resources cannot guarantee it. The dense, terraced streets of my remembered steel town in South Wales were poor but prosocial and happy in a way that the wealthy gated community depicted in Katherine Round's excellent documentary *The Divide* was not. It was as if the fabric of the old place eased neighbourliness.

In its reimagined twenty-first-century iteration, the acres of connected terraced streets are gone. People's homes have been disconnected from their town centre. And, while a covered market still exists for meeting, buying, bartering and chats (for me a place of boiled sweets and sixpences retrieved by work-worn fingers and thumbs from the leathery depths of women's purses), getting to it is a trial, across an inhuman, uninhabited highway. Although the market seemed to be doing OK (just) when I last visited, I was left wondering how much longer this part of the town's everyday heritage could realistically last.

We must begin to undo what we have done to places over the past half century if we are to tackle urban distress. We must make places that replace fret with chat. As much as there is a need to revive the built environment professions, so there is a need to support powerful community activity. I have argued elsewhere that if we are to make these vital changes, then our communities of place need themselves to become communities of interest.[3] Among a body of work conducted for the What Works Centre for Wellbeing with colleagues at the University of Liverpool and Leeds Beckett University, we have reviewed the evidence on the effects of joint decision-making in communities and of place and space infrastructure[4] on aspects or drivers of community well-being. This gives us an excellent foundation for future practice.

This evidence tells us, for example, that different 'interventions' in place seem to support different social capital outcomes. If we want to promote networks or local skills and knowledge, then community hubs may be the best option. While local events encourage cultural and heritage participation in a way that other interventions may not, our evidence review also demonstrates that interventions to improve the public realm are best at making communities feel safer and for boosting the local economy.

The important caveat to all of this is that improving the well-being of our communities seems only to appear as a result of a meaningful, involving process. Top-down imposition of 'interventions' in places does not work to improve well-being and nor do lean and mean, 'tick box' forms of engagement. In fact, our evidence shows that these forms of practice can lead to detrimental outcomes, increasing fret instead of encouraging chat. Meaningful involvement means sharing decisions in democratic open settings where dialogue is encouraged, and difference embraced and absorbed prior to consensus setting – where communities are involved from the outset and during every point of decision-making and implementation.

What does meaningful community involvement bring to the decisions themselves? Apart from grounded lived experience of the place, proper involvement is likely to shift the way we make decisions from a pessimistic problem-solving mindset to an optimistic solutions-focused one, in part because of the lived experience of the place through time and across activities. In our work we have found that concerted thinking about the future of places with others brought with it an inevitably optimistic frame of mind. After all, when we design and plan places we never purposefully plan for a worse future. Therefore, the design and governance of our places is a hopeful, future-oriented practice and, when done with others, it leads to consideration of outcomes beyond the egocentric, so encouraging a natural cooperative spirit and a grounded common concern, allowing community of place to become community of interest.

The re-thinking of community as we take action against urban distress should also consider how disciplinary communities and sector-based working may have deepened and prolonged the issues we face. The need to break down 'silos' is an often-heard cry whenever we consider the 'wicked' issues we face today. The unhelpful effects of these silos include mechanisms that sustain the divide between research, policy and practice, including the idea, again often heard from practitioners and policymakers, that academics make things unnecessarily complex. While it's true that jargon does little but muddle, the issues we need to consider are complex, and in order to address them with any likelihood of success we must embrace that complexity by adopting system approaches, looking to build evidence-informed policies that can withstand the inevitable turbulence of international, national and local politics.

For no one is all of this more important than for our children. It is acknowledged that most mental distress has its origins in childhood. It is thought that about half of all mental health issues emerge before the age of 14, climbing to three quarters by the age of 25. Daily we hear of the alarming increased prevalence of distress in young people and of the struggles that our current services, both educational and health, face as a result.[5] The scale of this issue already seems unmanageable and certainly any role of living environment professions can only be a piece in the jigsaw to address this grave concern. But, seen in the context of how a new narrative for planning can boost community well-being, we begin to see what an important component these professions play. Our urban children struggle to learn to live independent, autonomous lives that provide them with a sense of their own destiny because every outing they make is accompanied by parents, themselves too concerned with environmental threat to allow their children to walk to school, to play out or get to friends' houses by themselves.

If there is a golden rule in psychology it is that our behaviours and attitudes are, for the most part, learned. As young children we learn our anxieties from our parents, adding an intergenerational layer to urban distress. Part of changing our cities into flourishing places instead of anxious spaces must lie in how we prioritise children's needs in the urban environment. Play, until recently abjectly missing as an objective of urban strategy, must feature explicitly in any city framework or vision. For this reason, it is good to see ZCD architects with Westminster University embracing the views of children in their recent report *Neighbourhood Design: Working with Children towards a Child Friendly City* where they regard 'children as the generators of community life'.[6]

To get beyond warm words, the objectives that prioritise children's needs must be backed up by an agreed and inclusive governance model that enables the vision to become a daily reality of urban life. Failure to do this fails our children and ensures the continuation of urban anxiety into the future.

My remembered South Wales steel town was a place of cherished school holidays shared with grandparents, where between the terraces lay an overlooked, not very fancy, minimally maintained 'rec' (just a bombed out terrace then laid to grass, I now understand) where summers were spent playing out with the local kids, turning cartwheels, spinning on the railings till we were dizzy, catching elvers in the brook, eating rissoles from paper while watching the older kids break out from family into their grown-up world.

Today this playground is a distributor road.

To change the future to a better, more prosperous and contented one for those of us who live in towns and cities we must

1. Replace economic growth with growth of social capital as the chief objective of all policy
2. Understand how community well-being can be supported through policy and then enact those policies
3. Ensure that in the twenty-first century we prioritise young people through overarching, national strategies such as Wales's Wellbeing of Future Generations Act.

THE ANXIOUS CITY IS A COMPLICATED PLACE

Graham Marshall

People are complicated; cultures are complicated; cities are complicated. So let's embrace the complexity and eschew the simplistic expedient responses that make life harder. That's the route to good governance and a sustainable future.

When we consider the city in emotional terms we are talking about people, communities and societies – not the built environment. Anxiety ebbs and flows. Sometimes 'we have never had it so good'; in other times we are in national crisis. Anxiety discriminates – it's sexist, racist, homophobic, class-ridden and economic. There are differences in the way individual and collective anxieties are felt, their causes and impacts. Interestingly, anxiety is embedded in place and hidden in clear sight.

Here I reflect on the relationship between people and place following 30 years in practice as a placemaker. A practice that has made me anxious. Anxious that we continually fail to create places of thrival. Anxious at the democratic deficiency that prevents me from making a positive contribution to my own city in the United Kingdom. Anxiety that causes me to question urban theories, training and practice in the development and stewardship of our cities. With professional reflection, I return each time to the ecology of people and place; especially the evolutionary psychology that makes sense of our relationships and responses to each other, and to place. In this context we should appreciate 'anxiety' as a normal response to place, and chronic anxiety as a valid tipping point where we consider the effectiveness and consequences of our urban policymaking.

A little stress every day keeps us stimulated and alert; it also helps us learn and bond. Chronic anxiety makes us ill and changes our behaviours and relationships to both others and place. That in turn can change others' behaviour and the shape and function of places. Chronic individual and collective anxiety has been a feature of human life for millennia. The violent patriarchs from the Stone Age sometimes reflected in documentaries on apes; Viking raiders; Norman conquests; the Potato Famine in Ireland. All related to our needs as social animals, all related to geography, place and resources. Most importantly, all related to security. Importantly, these psychological responses are evolutionary in nature and normal in their contexts.

The idea of a 'current crisis' of urban anxiety has many facets, including perspective and perception. Thomas Gray's Elegy Written in a Country Churchyard in 1750 presents a thriving country life 'Far from the madding crowd's ignoble strife'. In 1874, Thomas Hardy published his anti-pastoral irony *Far from the Madding Crowd* depicting the economic precariousness of the countryside and lives full of strife. This dichotomy of perspective and perception is well illustrated in the studies of Raymond Williams on the recurring themes of people, country and cities throughout historic literature. This is important because the perspective taker needs to understand that their perception of what they see is not necessarily the same as the person habitually experiencing that place. The planner, architect, engineer and politician habitually apply their value judgements, often normative professional ones, without taking the time to appreciate a different perspective – without consulting the evidence. From this comes lazy thinking, repeated mistakes and a silo mentality to place stewardship.

The problem starts with exploitation. Our well-being depends upon us feeling good about ourselves. This can be hedonic well-being, which focuses on happiness and pain avoidance, and eudaemonic well-being which can be defined by the degree to which a person is fully functioning and satisfied. To be sustainable as individuals and communities we need a little of the former and a lot of the latter. When we are exploited, our well-being is compromised, making us more likely to grasp those hedonic hits that make us feel instantly better. This becomes cyclical with the hedonic offer becoming an exploitation itself. How many urban design masterplans focus on town and city centres? How many of those are oriented around retail and leisure, how many promote 'café culture' for the public realm, and how many high streets and centres are failing? Consider deprived cities like Liverpool and Krakow with their 'gig' economies, or Venice that has become a tourist resort and no longer a living city.

Disraeli put it this way:

> 'In great cities men are brought together by the desire of gain. They are not in a state of co-operation, but of isolation, as to the making of fortunes; and for all the rest they are careless of neighbours. [...] Two nations; between whom there is no intercourse and no sympathy; who are as ignorant of each other's habits, thoughts, and feelings, as if they were dwellers in different zones, or inhabitants of different planets; who are formed by a different breeding, are fed by a different food, are ordered by different manners, and are not governed by the same laws.' 'You speak of ...' said Egremont, hesitatingly, 'THE RICH AND THE POOR.'
>
> (From *Sybil*, Benjamin Disraeli (1845), Book II, ch. 5)[7]

The poor in the United Kingdom are an expanding precariat facing increasing inequalities and injustice through unstable, insecure labour, declining and volatile wages, loss of benefits and chronic indebtedness. Lack of occupational identity, anomie, alienation and disenchantment are perpetuating their chronic anxiety. The rate of change of these negative features of urban life has become more volatile in our contemporary times, sweeping up a greater proportion of the in-work and home-owning population, and threatening future generations with increasing impoverishment. When resources become scarce like this, it is difficult to plan for a future, promoting future-discounting behaviours in people who are encouraged and facilitated by hedonic gig economies. Alcohol, drug use, fast food, technological consumerism and addiction to social media become the fallbacks. This is recognised by Life History Theory, and exacerbated by the negative mental health outcomes intensified in cities and collectively known as the Urbanicity Effect. Together they generate a downward spiral that is hard to check or reverse because behaviours have become habituated.

Habituated is an interesting term. It refers to behaviour that is inextricably linked to a context or habitat – an environment; a place; a human ecosystem – reminding us that this behaviour is adaptive and not undesirable per se. It is not unusual to find impoverishment reflected in the built environment. From the quality of buildings and the services and facilities they accommodate, to the quality of the public realm, the stage set of our humanity, we are constantly reminded of our status and worth. These are the places where we forage and compete for resources according to Maslow's hierarchy of needs.

This ties the resilience of individuals and communities to the resilience of places. A weak place will be hit hard by an economic downturn and find it difficult to bounce back when the upturn arrives; a strong place will prevail and have the resource capacity to support its community. It is place resilience that makes the impact of economic change uneven. Resilient people cope well with life challenges, and when combined with resilient places, the less resilient are supported too. To overcome the anxious city, we need emancipatory cities where capital, revenue and intangible resources are of high quality, stable and accessible to all. Part of that intangible resource is pro-sociality where people look out for each other as social species must. These positive city attributes require appropriate physical spaces and stewardship to succeed.

Unfortunately, most people are 'place blind'. By that I mean they lack an appreciation of the impact that the quality of design and stewardship has on their lives. Throughout our work with communities we consistently find people have an idiocentric outlook about their environment, often feeling or believing it is somebody else's responsibility – usually an authority. Working through codesign sessions often transforms their outlook on place into an allocentric one. This real and perceived lack of control contrasts with our constant monitoring of the environments we forage through looking for resources and threat. This monitoring is instinctual, involving quick and dirty decision-making based on experience – our habitual choices. We know immediately if we like a place, if we'd fit in, if it has what we need and if it is safe. We immediately make inferences about people who inhabit new places and we love convenience. These natural and normal behaviours shape our places which in turn shape our behaviours. If we want to promote more sustainable behaviours, we need policies that support them. Policy must bring rationality to the myriad value judgements we all make about places.

Place stewardship is primarily a desk-based and remote activity undertaken by authorities and professionals at a strategic level, while people experience their places in the immediate small spaces they move through following various daily patterns. This disconnect is the source of people's idiocentric relationship with place, the lack of control contributing to their anxieties. If strategic planning is to be effective, it follows that decision-making should be based on an appreciation of the impact it has on the ground, and that natural incremental change continues beyond the scope of the strategy. It is these incremental changes that go unnoticed but erode places and negatively impact lives.

Perhaps the best illustration of this point is the impact transport planning has on people and places. Movement is fundamental to us; our foraging activities rely on this for work, collecting food and our social relationships. The scale of cities makes movement a very complex system, but to some extent it is as self-regulating as it is self-perpetuating and is dictated by basic principles and requirements. From the basic marketplace at a crossroads in a hamlet, movement patterns fundamentally shape all places through the public realm, which in turn shapes people. Transport planning, while strategic, cannot lose sight of this and must respect all the roles the public realm needs to fulfil to ensure places serve the people's needs. However, the greatest pressure against this is the unfettered accommodation of the private car. The negative impacts on the quality and functionality of the public realm are expressed in narrow pavements, interrupted desire lines, perceived and real dangers, and the pollution of the air with gasses and noise. The negative impacts on society are expressed in reduced density and diversity from critical mass and car dependency that discriminates against the majority. Most invidious is the impact on our essential social relationships, which greatly affects our well-being. This has been exacerbated by a rapidly growing trend for pavement parking, unthinkable previously, but a commonplace behaviour change at this time. Why do we put up with these unsustainable and selfish land uses? Because they provide convenience for many, another natural trait exploited in the name of the economy.

People often ask: 'Do you have any examples of a good place?' I would love to say yes and then extol their virtues, but the answer is no, I don't know of any contemporary places where there is not a precariat suffering for the benefit of others. You shouldn't measure a city by its richest street, but by its poorest.

Historically, cities evolved within inequitable and exploiting societies, though there were many positive aspects to their form through movement and trade patterns that supported our social needs. More recent urban development has focused on the car and a more fluid economy, not those wider social needs of the street. It is a different form of discrimination which has led to the erosion of traditional places to the extent that they have become dysfunctional for the purposes of well-being and social sustainability. In the past the 'anxious' precariat lived shorter, sicklier lives while society looked the other way. However, the peak of industrialisation brought a revolution in social responsibility, votes for all and a Welfare State. It is getting harder to turn that blind eye now in the social media revolution, and difficult not to realise that the anxious city harms all of us.

A good illustration of positive and impactful change that is scaleable from the hamlet to the cityscape is the regeneration of Poynton in Cheshire via a simple junction redesign – visit or watch the short film at https://tinyurl.com/y75rmf3e. Remembering that blind and disabled people are a precariat, I am putting aside accessibility issues for now to focus on the important messages at the end of the film. People are talking about social improvements and we can see prosocial behaviours emerging from a public realm design that is traditional in its form, but innovative in highway design terms. It's telling to note that road users are travelling at half the speed, in half the road space, in half the time their journeys used to take through the town. This civilisation of highways into spaces and streets has led to an economic uplift.

If we want to overcome the anxious city and make cities places of thrival, we need to stand back and take a hard look at our repetitive mistakes. We especially need to look at the lives of the precariat, the disempowered recipients of the shortest straw, to develop a truly civilised and humanitarian ethos for our placemaking. As an unapologetic exponent of the 1999 Urban Renaissance in the United Kingdom, I believe that we must regather the momentum this generated and return proactive place stewardship to the top of our national agenda. Reactive problem-solving – 'sink estates'; healthy new towns; high streets – sidesteps the point that the performance of the whole habitat relies on the stewardship of the whole habitat for communities to be viable. This brings us back to the point that the anxious city is a complex place and simplistic problem-solving approaches tend to make things worse. That is called future discounting.

The adage that Rome wasn't built in a day is apt. We need big ambitions for our future places and communities, but big masterplans and strategies are seldom fulfilled. We need a stepwise approach framed around an ethos that puts the safeguarding of social sustainability front and centre in the stewardship of existing towns and cities. The intensification of existing places to deliver social sustainability should be a priority, and from that we can generate an appropriate rationale for new settlements and extensions that are not car-dependant and toxic to well-being.

For me, the first three steps in this journey, which are strategic, local and flexible enough to complement evolving government policy, are to promote these three principles in our towns and cities:

1. Social value – put social sustainability at the heart of all policymaking and assess all public funding and action in the public realm against social outcomes.
2. Co-production – put people at the heart of place stewardship and involve them in the co-production of new projects and the management and maintenance of their local environments.
3. Place directorates – remove the silos within local authorities and rebuild officer teams around balanced placemaking principles and a social ethos.

Notes

1. M. Lewicka, 'Place Attachment: How Far Have We Come in the Last 40 Years?', *Journal of Environmental Psychology* 31 (2011): 207–30. Accessed 17 April 2020. https://www.sciencedirect.com/science/article/abs/pii/S0272494410000861.
2. R. Corcoran and G. Marshall, 'Planning for Wellbeing', *Journal of Urban Design and Mental Health*, 1 (2016): 5. Accessed 17 April 2020. https://www.urbandesignmentalhealth.com/journal1-planning4wellbeing.html.
3. R. Corcoran, 'Academic Perspective: When Communities of Place Become Communities of Interest: The Magic Catalyst of Community Wellbeing?'. What Works Centre for Wellbeing, 27 August 2017. Accessed 17 April 2020. https://whatworkswellbeing.org/blog/academic-perspective-when-communities-of-place-become-communities-of-interest-the-magic-catalyst-of-community-wellbeing/.
4. Ibid.
5. 'Mental Health: 'Primary School Head Teachers Speak Out about Lack of Support'. BBC News, 18 July 2019. Accessed 17 April 2020. https://www.bbc.co.uk/news/av/education-49018831/mental-health-primary-school-head-teachers-speak-out-about-lack-of-support.
6. ZCD Architects, 'Neighbourhood Design: Working with Children towards a Child Friendly City'. Accessed 17 April 2020. https://static1.squarespace.com/static/58aaff9b17bffc6029da965f/t/5c6aa00b53450ac8afadc635/1550491676571/Neighbourhood+Design.pdf.
7. Disraeli, Benjamin, *Sybil, or, the Two Nations* (Oxford: Oxford University Press, [1845] 2017).

Chapter 5

THE VIOLENT CITY

VIOLENCE IN THE CITY: INEQUALITY, INTIMIDATION AND FEAR

Elizabeth Cook and Anthony Ellis

Locating Violence in the City

Today, violence is an issue that is difficult to ignore or to avoid. Evidence of it is seemingly everywhere: violence receives prevalent coverage in the 24-hour news media and it is also pervasive within our popular culture, such as in film, television and literature. There is a similarly vast amount of policy and academic literature that addresses violence in historical, comparative and theoretical contexts. The problem of violence is one that is frequently considered to be synonymous with large cities. In particular, certain neighbourhoods within cities often have reputations as dangerous places and can become spaces of both fear and fascination. While prevalent, and at times sensationalist, coverage of violence in the media can create a sense of fear that does not match the risks of experiencing violence in the city, it remains a fact that risks are not distributed evenly. Some groups are at much greater risk than others, and in British cities today, violence is a genuine and persistent issue in some neighbourhoods.

Although crime in Britain has been in decline for over two decades, *violent* crime has started to see real rises and to have a hugely detrimental impact, particularly within more excluded urban communities, now figuring highly on the political and public agenda. Between 2017 and 2018, a total of 285 people were killed by use of a knife or sharp instrument, the highest number recorded in a year since 1946 when the Home Office started recording the number of murders committed annually.[1] Much of this recent violence has been concentrated in particular areas of large cities including London, Birmingham and Liverpool. These are cities with sometimes vibrant economies and considerable wealth, but which also retain large, disconnected and under-resourced communities for whom few policies or programmes have been designed or devoted for over ten years now. Many such areas remain poor, with low-quality and under-resourced public services that have been made considerably worse by austerity measures over this period.

The increase in violence has been accompanied by considerable concern from the media and politicians regarding what some see as a kind of 'epidemic' of knife violence afflicting some of Britain's major urban centres, with talk of 'blood-soaked streets'. In response, the British prime minister Boris Johnson announced additional funding for the Crown Prosecution Service, an additional 10,000 prison places and a toughening of sentencing guidelines to tackle rising rates of violent offending. While there is evidence that 'higher harm' forms of violent offending are increasing in particular parts of some British cities, the media frenzy that surrounds this issue obscures and disguises a range of structural factors that continue to remain peripheral to policy debates addressing the causes and potential solutions.

Cities are not intrinsically violent places, but they contain spaces and conditions that, in particular combinations, can generate violence. This can be highlighted by the considerable variations in the shape and trends of violence both between and within cities. We tend to find few voices in the public domain questioning the presence of violence in our cities. However, it is clear from many years of research on these issues that violence is unevenly distributed across the sub-areas of cities and often in close parallel to the distribution of forms of social marginalisation and disenfranchisement which have blended to create excluded, contained and so-called dangerous communities.

There are sections of cities which continue to be subject to various coercive policies of aggressive stop-and-search and 'hotspot' policing tactics, many of which sit closely alongside much more affluent neighbourhoods that have become increasingly securitised and gated. Trends in knife violence, which have had the gravest effects on young men in certain communities, have appeared alongside the evacuation of key welfare and institutional supports – including the loss of many youth clubs, Sure Start programs, social work and other youth diversion provisions. While these communities have become designated 'hotspots' for aggressive policing strategies, much of the media and political talk regarding crime and violence has become heavily racialised. The effect of this has often been to obscure the role of inequality and the loss of social and economic protections as key factors that help us to understand these problems.

An obsession with the 'dangerous streets' often identified as the backdrop for these events has also perhaps skewed our focus away from the threats found within the presumably 'safe haven of the home'. Between 2017 and 2018, more than a million women in England and Wales reported being a victim of domestic abuse.[2] Further analysis reveals the tendency among victims not to report such incidents, which highlights that this figure is likely to be a significant underestimate. The considerable attention that has been directed towards 'public' violence between young men on Britain's city streets draws our gaze from this heavily gendered violence against women from men known to them, which receives a very different political response.

Understanding Violence in the City

To think of violence as purely a product of the culture of those that are confined to the margins creates a fallacy that this is a 'subcultural' or pathological issue, one isolated from the rest of society. Furthermore, such an approach focuses upon violence as a solely physical act perpetrated by individuals. This draws our attention away from the systematic trends of brutality that lie behind more insidious processes of capitalism that connect geographies of inequality, exclusion and violence. What seems to be a connection between violent *acts* – the tangible, extraordinary and spectacular violence – and violent *processes* – the endemic and embedded violence – is however somewhat difficult to unpack. We should nevertheless pay more attention to how violent *processes* of austerity, the dismantling of social welfare and growing inequality filter down into the lived realities of vulnerability and fear that characterise violent *acts* unfolding in many cities today.

Many of those caught up in what is being termed an 'epidemic' of urban violence are confined to specific sub-geographies of British cities that rely more heavily upon public services and amenities that have been starved of investment and stripped down by years of austerity cuts: youth projects that have been closed, leaving groups of young people with fewer positive provisions and activities; cuts to early intervention services to support children at risk of abuse; fewer services and hostels to house and protect women who are victims of domestic abuse; fewer police officers to respond to violent and offending behaviour that has detrimental effects on communal life; and the 'vigilante' groups and local 'hard men' popping up in some of these sub-geographies to fill the void. These cuts arrived on the back of decades of economic restructuring in Britain that fundamentally altered traditional labour markets, fractured and weakened workers' movements, and led to greater economic inequality. With options that mostly consist of low-paid, insecure forms of work, amid the ubiquity of images of desirable consumer products and lifestyles, and the wealthy groups who possess them, considerable numbers of people are now living out their lives with little hope or optimism.

For some young males in particular who are confined to particular marginalised sub-geographies of British cities, the success of some local organised criminals and drug dealers provides evidence of a viable, potentially lucrative alternative to zero-hours contracts, minimum wages, unsocial hours, and the ignominy of employment in the low-level service economy. With diminished options for gaining and maintaining self-respect, violence can become for some disenfranchised and poor men a means of acquiring respect and making their way in a competitive and potentially dangerous criminal economy.

The increasing incidents of serious violence recorded and reported during the past several years are partly a reflection of a culture that promotes individualism and celebrates consumer competence in a broader context of inequality that creates significant disadvantages and limits opportunities, alongside the declining presence of services in some communities that can protect citizens. Such feelings of insecurity and vulnerability may also speak to the problem of declining trust in police and faith in local authorities to provide protection. The withdrawal of welfare does not stop at social and economic support, but extends to a lack of protection and security provided by police who share poor relations with some communities – relations that have been further aggravated by the hostile treatment of minority groups through over-policing.

Physical *acts* of violence, that are pushing up violent crime figures, are difficult to detach from the harmful consequences of economic crises and poorly thought-out political decisions. Despite these connections the media and politicians continue to focus solely upon the exceptional and more easily quantifiable forms of public violence involving marginalised groups of young men, which leaves these structural conditions unaddressed. To quote Danny Dorling[3] at length:

> Behind the man with the knife is the man who sold him the knife, the man who did not give him a job, the man who decided that his school did not need funding, the man who closed down the branch plant where he could have worked, the man who decided to reduce benefit levels so that a black economy grew. […] The harm done to one generation has repercussions long after that harm is first acted out.

There is a slow process of violence that unfolds here which cannot be detached from matters of uneven economic transformation and austerity which create fear and insecurity for particular groups. However, these vulnerabilities present themselves differently across the city and unfold gradually over time. The challenge is to remain sensitive to the gender, class and geographical features of contemporary violence across the city without conflating the solutions that different violences require.

Responding to Violence in the City

It is important to acknowledge that there are continuities between these violences that transgress different 'public' and 'private' spaces in the city, all the while garnering different levels of political attention and action. To talk of precariousness in the city should therefore take note of the different spaces in which these vulnerabilities unfold not only in terms of sub-geography, gender and class, but also in terms of how they accumulate over time. We hope that the following efforts listed below provide some response and optimism for moving forward in responses to violence in the city.

1. Economic reinvestment in local and national services. This is needed to manage, respond and prevent violence in cities, redressing the impact of budget cuts which have had a lasting impact on charities for the homeless, women's refuges, community centres, and police, probation and prisons.
2. Listen to families and communities by encouraging the active participation of local communities in decision-making about the solutions and perceived obstacles to reducing violence.
3. Develop collaborative partnerships and integrate them into public policy through a network of agencies working collaboratively. Address violence holistically through joint working by support services in housing, education, family, employment and health using shared agendas and approaches.

Economic Reinvestment in Local and National Services

The concerted withdrawal of city resources aimed at managing, responding to and preventing violence in cities has become a significant obstacle in the effort to reduce violence. It is important that politicians and policy makers reinvest in services that have seen consistent budget cuts. These cuts have had a lasting impact on all forms of services from charities for the homeless, women's refuges and community centres and other welfare services to police, probation and prisons. The cuts to these services have a particularly violent effect on the most vulnerable of communities, which non-profit charities also struggle to support as funding cuts create the pressure of competition and threaten the risk of closure. If resources were driven back into these services, we could hope to see people in marginalised and vulnerable communities with renewed access to support and opportunity and better ability to seek safety.

This economic reinvestment might also extend to re-establishing shared public, creative spaces which different communities feel safe in and confident in accessing. It seems that as the number of public spaces declines there is less opportunity for meaningful exchange and more opportunity for fears for personal safety and insecurity to emerge. While some key groups are consistently excluded from participation in certain spaces, others have sought to limit the free use of parks, squares and centres. As more shared, creative spaces become more available and accessible to people, we hope that more opportunities emerge for collaborative debates from the ground.

Democratic Decision-Making: Listen to Families and Communities

Closely linked to the promise of economic investment is the importance of renewing a sense of confidence in political leadership. The current climate is marked by uncertainty and ambiguity in politics which has experienced changes in leadership, decision-making and policies almost on a day-by-day basis, fuelling a growing disconnect between people and politics. Many are increasingly disillusioned in the ability of authorities, particularly the police, to protect citizens and, in some communities, are fearful of the efforts of stop-and-search and other aggressive surveillance tactics. More attention should be placed on encouraging the active participation of local communities in decision-making about the solutions and perceived obstacles to reducing violence.

Much better provision should be made available for these services to support and empower local communities to participate in debates on violence in cities. This would involve talking *to* rather than *about* or *around* those most affected by these events and ultimately avoid stigmatising those who are already in vulnerable positions. This requires listening to families and communities and, rather than laying responsibility at their door and treating them as suspects, paying attention to what they consider to be the best ways of moving forward for *their* community.

Shared Agendas: Collaborative Partnerships and Integration into Public Policy

We have highlighted in this discussion that violence in cities is not, and should not, be the responsibility of one authority or body. Rather it should be the concern of a network of agencies that work collaboratively, speaking across rather than down to one another. The response to violence touches upon issues of economic and social exclusion, fear, insecurity and vulnerability, which require the attention not only of criminal justice agencies, but of public health, education and welfare ones too (we note, too, the massive cuts to such bodies). This is an idea that has been gathering increasing pace in recent discussions of public health approaches to violence trialled in both Glasgow and London in recent years. This approach focuses on a holistic approach to violence which situates it within broader dynamics within and across communities and both economic and social conditions. This requires a cross-sectoral approach where support services in housing, education, family, employment and health work together using shared agendas and approaches to violence. If violence prevention was incorporated into broader public policies there would be better recognition of the economic and social insecurities and vulnerabilities that precede violence as well as a better understanding of the wider impacts of violence in cities.

MATTERING AND THE VIOLENCE IN OUR CITIES

Luke Billingham and Keir Irwin-Rogers

Every day, across the United Kingdom, young people are told that they don't matter. Rarely in so many words, yet many of the key adults, authorities and institutions in young people's lives convey exactly this message, by, for example, evicting families from their homes; excluding young people from school (or dumping them in 'isolation'); denying them dignified work opportunities (or any work at all); roughly and disrespectfully stop-and-searching them; failing to properly treat their mental health problems or addictions (or those of their parents); treating them as stereotypes; criminalising them; throwing them in unsafe, unsanitary prisons; refusing them any hope of housing in their community; closing their youth centres; transforming their area without consulting them; neglecting to address domestic violence in their homes; defunding their schools; reducing their welfare payments; treating them as a problem to be solved; or, almost as damagingly, subtly belittling them, in countless insidious ways. It may not need saying that we view this neglect and persistent denigration of young people as fundamental to wider problems in our cities, including violence.

In the context of massive funding cuts, many services and agencies aimed at young people are either closing down or have become so transactional and punitive that they serve to constrain and discipline rather than support and encourage. Whether we view institutions, like schools and the police, as authoritarian or as potentially beneficial for young people, austerity has rendered them increasingly unforgiving and cold. A significant proportion of our young people experience overt hostility and a lack of support in the neighbourhoods they live in and the services they access. Far too many experience a toxic combination of factors that exclude and demoralise. Those afflicted by these multiple forms of marginalisation are most concentrated in our urban areas, whether this be in our major conurbations, coastal communities or post-industrial towns.

Jake: A Precarious Sense of Mattering

We can bring these forces to life by considering examples from our own experience of working with young people in East London. One 18-year-old boy, who we'll call Jake, has been systematically diminished more or less since birth. His mother does her very best, but has been neglected by men in her life who should have given her more support, while also struggling with her mental health problems and chronic financial need. She loves Jake deeply, and communicates this to him often, but she has problems with drugs, finds supporting Jake very difficult, and sometimes snaps, badly. Jake has spent time in care. They now have housing problems and he has been permanently excluded from the local school – a purpose-built academy sponsored by a large multinational company which has a 'zero-tolerance' approach to bad behaviour. After the exclusion, Jake went to an Alternative Provision (AP) school which he described as unsafe, and which terrified his mum. Relevant professionals offered advocacy for Jake, and he was moved into a more suitable AP school. Shortly after this, Jake was subjected to an aggressive stop-and-search by the police. This happened because he was riding a bike that the police thought was stolen and thought that he could not afford. His aunt had recently bought it for him as a gift.

Jake dabbled in County Lines drug dealing, which is where young people become involved in drug distribution networks beyond the city, to rural areas and other towns. This can be a lucrative trade for young people, or can appear so, though it involves exploitation by more senior dealers and the ever-present risk of violence, arrest or both. It can be appealing for young people in the context of low and insecure employment, and even more so for those excluded from education, who have few other opportunities for respect or resource.

Thankfully, Jake has not been directly involved in interpersonal violence himself, though he has carried a weapon, and says he has almost been compelled to use it. The walls of Jake's house are pockmarked with holes, where he's punched them in anger and frustration. So far, his simmering rage has been largely restricted to explosive family rows, but there is concern among professionals that it could boil over onto the street.

Jake's story is complex and punctuated by hope, despite the difficulty of his context. He has been lucky to have the support of an excellent National Health Service (NHS) psychologist and has been well supported by the staff in the new AP. He has also recently completed a finance course with a tutor who has come from a similar background and who's gone on to become a mentor.

Jake is intelligent, sharp, funny and strong, but his potential has been inadequately tapped. He has heard the message that he does not matter loud and clear, all too often. His faith and trust in adults, institutions and authorities has been eroded and his sense of personal alienation is palpable. He does not have a secure sense of his value – he says that young people like him 'feel useless'. This is not just a feeling, but in a way reflects reality: far from the (legitimate) labour market, kicked out of school, dependent on an ever-more punitive welfare system, there is a sense in which Jake and others like him do not matter to the country's political economy, or only matter in the sense that they are a problem to be dealt with.

For young people to grow up differently to Jake, structures and institutions need to change: we need fewer families in poverty, fewer communities riven by inequality, fewer funding cuts to education and services, and more warmth and patience in our schools. But such needs are the exact opposite of where we have been going for over a decade in the communities we have been working with.

The Crisis of Mattering

Far too many young people are living lives similar to Jake's, or worse. Many people living in cities are going through what we would describe as a crisis of mattering. A wide variety of factors conspire to undermine individuals' sense of significance and agency. It's never been easier to feel unimportant, and this is particularly acute for young people. Ask any (fortunate) adult what makes them feel they matter, and their answer will probably include lots of things that young people don't yet have, and may have very little hope of attaining: their job, their home, their children, their responsibilities, their published writings and so on.

The generational divide is significant – young people's lives in the United Kingdom today are in many cases characterised by insecurity and precariousness which far exceeds that experienced by previous post-war generations. This condition is most acute for those who live in areas that have been hollowed out by deindustrialisation stretching back decades and by cuts to public services. Their communities have evidently mattered less than others to national decision-makers. These entrenched structural problems can be experienced on an individual level as a profound lack of mattering – a debilitating sense of impotence and insignificance in the social and political world. Figure 5.1 summarises some the forces which undermine people's sense that they matter. For those worst affected by these forces, intersecting cultural, political, economic and institutional factors leave them with very little sense of agency, significance, or hope. Critically, these forces come down most forcefully on particular districts of our towns and cities, and the vulnerable within them.

What It Means to Matter, and How This Relates to Violence

There is a growing literature on mattering, especially in the United States. It's been defined as 'the perception that [...] we are a significant part of the world around us'[4] and 'the belief that one makes a difference in the lives of others'.[5] As these definitions imply, there is both a social and an instrumental aspect to mattering: a need to feel significant to others, and to feel able to have some effect on the world. The need to matter is fundamental. We have a deep-seated need to matter to other people, and to matter in the physical world – to be a significant causal force in both a social and material sense. Our yearning to achieve belonging, status, respect and agency could be seen as an extension of these basic needs.

Institutional factors	Economic factors
School exclusions & rigid/cold approach to discipline	Inequality & poverty
Transactional rather than relational services	Austerity Poor job prospects
	Strain on families
	Housing problems
Stereotyping & discrimination	Low paid, precarious work
Cultural factors	**Political factors**
Decline of community?	Political instability & uncertainty
Decline of religion?	Gentrification Globalisation
Increasingly insecure relationships?	The ideology of meritocracy
Individualism/atomisation	Lack of voice, depoliticisation

Figure 5.1. Categorisation of factors undermining people's sense of value

Numerous studies have linked the frustration of these fundamental needs to violence. The feeling that you don't matter has both 'anti-social' and 'self-destructive' consequences:[6] the former involves aggressive assertions of personal significance through harming others, the latter involves destroying a self which has become intolerably diminished. What another author calls 'anti-mattering'[7] can create a sense of nihilism: lacking any sense of significance, individuals can fall into a state of normlessness or meaninglessness, devaluing both their own lives and those of others. This is not about individual pathology and violent individuals, rather it is fostered by the societal structures which systematically deny marginalised people recognition, respect and resource. Violence and street crime can provide a means through which people seek to satisfy these universal needs, and to avoid a feeling of worthlessness or what some call social death. The search for respect and recognition through violence forces others to register their existence and their causal power, even if this is in the form of moral judgement, fear or resentment.

Feeling that we don't matter appears to be a psychological result of marginalisation within 'mainstream' society, and there are all too many (semi-)organised groups of exploiters who will happily offer a whole new world of mattering and meaning to marginalised young people: often attached to illicit trades, particularly in the drug economy. Such people can become a substitute family, giving some young people a deep sense of belonging and status – provided they carry out orders. Of course, not all violence in cities is caused by those involved in some kind of organised criminal group; there are more individualised acts of violence taking place. But their nihilism and brutality can often still be linked to a broader struggle for mattering. Physically harming another person can produce a feeling of intoxicating potency, especially if you've been completely denied agency from an early age.

Our fear is that the violence we're witnessing on our cities' streets is caused, at least in part, by people who are struggling to acquire the material and the meaning they need to live a life that feels worthwhile or significant; a life that seems to matter. We're not sure how much the 'mainstream' of our society has to offer such people, and they have very little to lose as a result – growing up in contexts that offer few alternatives and which systematically degrade and demoralise young people.

Hope, Possibility and Change

If our political economy, culture and institutions continue to undermine our most marginalised people, it will be incredibly difficult for things to get better. Yet there remains hope that we can improve these outcomes. There are highly skilled and deeply dedicated people doing incredible work across the country to help inspire in people a rich, meaningful sense that they are valued. Youth and community centres nationwide (those we still have) provide a second home and a shedload of love. The best city schools nurture students' passion for knowledge and learning, but they also provide a warm, supportive environment, informed by a rich understanding of attachment, relationship-building and trauma, shot through with mutual respect. There are individual professionals in our schools, hospitals, charities, prisons, social care systems, and mental health services who help transform people's sense of themselves, and genuinely reorient their lives. There are community groups, activists and politicians fighting for the deeper, broad-ranging structural changes that are necessary if we are to properly rectify the grotesque inequality, poverty and marginalisation that blights our society. We need more of both: more places and professionals to nurture our most vulnerable people; and more radical change to reduce the hardship and demoralisation that are at the root of most social problems. The former without the latter would just be sticking plasters on a gaping wound; the latter without the former would be a cold kind of revolution.

Reflections on the Way Forward

Universal Basic Income and the Economic Foundation of Mattering

If implemented in the right way, Universal Basic Income could mean that people are no longer wholly dependent on selling themselves in the labour market – it could 'decommodify' people.⁸ One major cause of violence is too many people struggling with 'marginal work', which denies their dignity and exacerbates their marginalisation.⁹ Too many people have jobs that frustrate or deny their need to matter, working for organisations in which their existence makes a negligible difference. These 'bullshit jobs' are 'so completely pointless, unnecessary, or pernicious that even the employee cannot justify its existence'.¹⁰ If Universal Basic Income can significantly reduce the urgency of finding a job, it could hopefully bring about a new era of dignity and respect in the workplace, and – closely tied to this – fundamentally tip the balance of power away from employers and towards employees.

Debate of course rages about the viability, desirability and effectiveness of Universal Basic Income, but it can also, as shown in many of its implemented examples in Europe, help to insulate young people against being exploited.

Genuine Political Empowerment for All: Mattering Politically

Citizens, including those under voting age, need to have genuine political power – in a democracy everyone should matter politically. Rampant privatisation has taken far too many issues out of the realm of public, democratic decision-making, undermining our hope and trust in politics. The politics of our era has seemed more responsive to 'the markets' than the citizenry. Top-down 'regeneration' initiatives based on dubious notions of trickle-down economics disempower the very communities they are meant to benefit; academisation renders schools wholly unaccountable to any democratic local body.

Projects such as Citizens' Assemblies, and, in a very different way, the Occupy movement, have been attempts to provide people with actual power to influence decision-making. We need more thoroughgoing and sustainable initiatives than these.

At the city neighbourhood level, there are schemes which give local people real, meaningful decision-making power over how their area is changing. There are charities across the United Kingdom that do this brilliantly with young people, supporting them not only to design new community spaces, but also to build them – power tools and all. At best, projects such as these help marginalised people to realise that they can be world-makers: *they* can craft physical spaces (or organisations, or ideas) which *other* people can benefit from and use, rather than living their life surrounded by a built environment (and laws, norms, traditions and ideas) universally designed and created by other people, who generally look and sound nothing like them, and whose life experience is most often utterly remote from theirs. Finding small pots of cash to invest in these kinds of projects could pay real dividends.

Provision for New Parents: Supporting Families to Nurture a Healthy Sense of Mattering

Even for those with plentiful social and economic capital, the experience of caring for babies and bringing up young children can involve enormous difficulties. For those bringing children into the world in far more disadvantageous and complex circumstances, the experience can be terrifying, and can cause levels of stress, tension and discord which cause lasting damage to all in the family. In worst cases, neglect or abuse can leave children with a profound sense that they do not matter, even to their primary caregivers. This can lead to all kinds of negative consequences later in life, including an increased propensity to harm the self and others.

New parents and families need much more and much better support. Money should be flooding the services that surround new babies and their parents. Call these services Sure Start, Better Start, Flying Start, Delightful Start, whatever, but make them amazing and make sure they reach every new parent in the country. Train and retain inspirational professionals to work in this area and give them the pay and working conditions they need in order to provide the highest level of support. Empower them to build relationships of genuine care with the families they work with. The Buurtzorg model of social care in the Netherlands includes many of these elements, and of course there were many highly effective aspects of Sure Start before it was cut. Pen Green in Corby provides an inspirational example of excellence in care and education for small children.

If these three changes were made, we think there would be a whole raft of positive consequences, including a significant, 'downstream' reduction of violence in our cities. We think they would help to provide everybody with the sense – however intangible – that they matter.

Notes

1 Office for National Statistics. *Domestic Abuse in England and Wales: Year Ending March 2018* (London: ONS, 2018). Accessed 17 April 2020. https://www.ons.gov.uk/peoplepopulationandcommunity/crimeandjustice/bulletins/domesticabuseinenglandandwales/yearendingmarch2018#prevalence-of-domestic-abuse.
2 Office for National Statistics. *The Nature of Violent Crime in England and Wales: Year Ending March 2018* (London: ONS, 2019). Accessed 17 April 2020. https://www.ons.gov.uk/peoplepopulationandcommunity/crimeandjustice/articles/thenatureofviolentcrimeinenglandandwales/yearendingmarch2018.
3 D. Dorling, 'Prime Suspect: Murder in Britain', in *Criminal Obsessions: Why Harm Matters More Than Crime*, ed. D. Dorling et al., 2nd edn (London: Centre for Crime and Justice Studies, 2008).

4   G. C. Elliott, S. Kao and A. Grant, 'Mattering: Empirical Validation of a Social-Psychological Concept', *Self and Identity* 3 (2004): 339–54.
5   G. C. Elliott, M. Colangelo and R. J. Gelles, 'Mattering and Suicide Ideation: Establishing and Elaborating a Relationship', *Social Psychology Quarterly* 68(3) (2005): 223–38.
6   G. C. Elliott, *Family Matters: The Importance of Mattering to Family in Adolescence* (West Sussex: Wiley-Blackwell, 2009).
7   G. Flett, *The Psychology of Mattering: Understanding the Human Need to Be Significant* (London: Academic Press, 2018).
8   G. Standing, *Basic Income: And How We Can Make It Happen* (London: Pelican, 2017).
9   E. Currie, *The Roots of Danger* (Oxford: Oxford University Press, 2016).
10 D. Graeber, *Bullshit Jobs* (Harmondsworth: Penguin, 2018).

Chapter 6

THE SICK CITY

DO BLACK LIVES MATTER IN POLLUTED CITIES?

Bethany Thompson

Air pollution has become Britain's silent public health emergency. Air pollution can be defined as the presence in or introduction into the air of a substance that can be harmful or have poisonous effects on health. Public health research has shown a strong link between air quality and a person's quality of life. It is becoming increasingly apparent that there are complex connections between urban air pollution and the prevalence of health inequalities. Deep-rooted social structures perpetuate health inequalities through environmental injustices, sharpening racial disparities. This chapter will explore and challenge environmental factors which damage public health, and recommend realistic actionable steps to combat these challenges and the heavy burden they place on health services. The focus will be on urban air quality, exploring how race and ethnicity can affect health outcomes.

Racial and Social Inequalities within Urban Communities

As a Black health policy researcher, it has become increasingly evident to me that there are striking race disparities among the population of Britain when considering the effects of poor air quality. Research conducted in London shows that Black communities are disproportionately likely to breathe illegal levels of air pollution compared with their white and Asian counterparts.[1] This is an environmental injustice: African and Caribbean people account for 15.5 per cent of Londoners exposed to nitrogen dioxide, but only 13 per cent of the city's population. Such evidence poses the question, do Black lives matter in this instance? There are clear links between economically deprived areas and greater exposure to polluted air. In London boroughs such as Southwark, Lambeth and Hackney, there is a correlation between a high proportion of Black residents and high levels of pollution.

Table 6.1. Air pollution levels (micrograms per cubic metre) in cities with significant Black populations

City	Black population	Air pollution level
Manchester	8.6%	13
Liverpool	2.6%	12
Leicester	6.3%	12

Nitrogen dioxide (NO_2) is a harmful gas that can increase the likelihood of respiratory problems and cause significant harm for those with asthma, especially children and older people with chronic illnesses. Illegal levels of NO_2 can have significant impacts on human health. Public Health England's 'modelling framework' in 2017 showed that there were 60,648 incidences of disease attributable to NO_2 in England.[2] Poor air quality also contributes to days off sick from work, with an impact on the economy. In 2012, the Department for Environment, Food and Rural Affairs reported that poor air quality cost the economy £2.7 billion through its impact on productivity.[3] As Black people are more likely to live and work in urban areas with poor air quality, these figures are also evidence of social and racial inequality. Growing up Black in London, it can be argued, puts you at an unfair risk of the environmental hazards that contribute to health disparities.

Unless we address the structural inequalities that act as a catalyst for environmental injustices, society will continue to generate poor health outcomes for people living in urban environments. There is an increasing need to tackle environmental racism – the concentration of people from lower socio-economic backgrounds in urban areas that are home to a higher proportion of people from ethnic minorities.[4]

Road transport is a massive contributor to NO_2 pollution, disproportionately affecting people who live near busy roads in urban areas. The effects include, but are not limited to, asthma, cardiovascular disease, reduced lung function development, lung function decline and lung cancer. The UK Health Forum and Imperial College London state that a reduction in fine particulate air pollution in England could prevent '50,900 cases of coronary heart disease, 16,500 strokes, 9,300 cases of asthma and 4,200 lung cancers over an 18-year period'.[5] With the uneven distribution of ethnic minorities in urban areas, environmental injustices create a racial challenge to public health.

Table 6.1 shows three cities that are among the worst affected by air pollution in Britain alongside the percentage of Black residents. The World

Health Organisation states that air pollution levels should not exceed 10 micrograms per cubic metre, and all three cities exceed this level.[6]

Case Study: Ella Kissi-Debrah

Britain's environmental injustices and social inequalities are highlighted in the case of Ella Kissi-Debrah, a 9-year-old girl whose death from asthma was the first to be linked to air pollution. Ella Kissi-Debrah died in February 2013 after experiencing three years of seizures.[7] During this time, local air pollution in Lewisham, south London, where she lived, regularly breached EU legal limits. The inquest into her death revealed that she died of acute respiratory failure and severe asthma. Although her death may be the first recorded as caused by air pollution, it is estimated that 28,000 to 36,000 deaths in the United Kingdom are a result of manmade air pollution each year.

The Impact on Health Services

The rise in the number of people with poor health outcomes as a result of poor urban air quality places a heavy burden on health and social care services (both primary and secondary). Factors such as increased hospital admissions and accident and emergency visits compound the burden on scarce resources and healthcare professionals. Research from Kings College London and Imperial College found that on average four people in London (including one child) are hospitalised every day due to asthma caused by air pollution. Poor air quality leads to roughly one thousand hospital admissions for asthma and serious lung conditions in London each year.[8] It also adds to the demand for appointments with GPs and specialists who are the first point of contact for those with severe pollution-related health problems. The greatest burdens will be on health services in the most deprived urban areas, adding to the stress on services for all patients in these locations. The financial burden for the NHS runs into billions: the House of Commons Environment Audit Committee stated that the cost of health impacts of poor air quality was likely to exceed estimates of £8–20 billion.[9]

Overall, the public health effects of urban inequalities continue to be exacerbated by deep-rooted racial structures. The intersection between air pollution, health and socio-economic inequalities is not new, but raises important questions about disparities in public health. The fact that those living in the most deprived areas experience worse air quality[10] creates a divide in society and entrenches environmental injustices, adding to the pressures on primary and secondary health services.

While it is challenging to reduce the changes required to three ideas, even one change, however small, could have long-term positive impacts. Below I recommend three actionable ideas to improve community well-being, which I then explain further.

1. Work towards dismantling structural inequalities
2. Encourage diversity in 'White spaces'
3. Educate people on how to fight for basic human rights

Work towards Dismantling Structural Inequalities

Tackling structural inequalities first is key. Those in a position of privilege have a duty to dismantle structural inequalities. Poor health outcomes are not only down to the individual's lifestyle, but also a result of Britain's unequal balance of quality of life. MPs representing urban constituencies and others in positions of power should recognise and combat environmental racism by advocating for the human rights of those who live in polluted areas. In doing so, they should work with local communities to push for top-down changes to change structures that influence air pollution (such as transport and planning policies). Citizens who have the privilege of living in less polluted areas must aid this work by advocating for government pledges to tackle the environmental injustices and social structures that sustain public health disparities. Those who benefit from privilege need to understand that poor air quality is a collective problem: although it affects urban environments most, its impacts are felt across health services.

Encourage Diversity in 'White Spaces'

We need to encourage diversity in open green spaces. The term 'White space' can be defined as a place where the norm is to see white people rather than ethnic minorities. Time spent in less polluted spaces could help to reduce exposure to the effects of unhealthy air, so encouraging ethnic minorities to occupy open green spaces which are often seen as 'White spaces' could gradually help to decrease health gaps between ethnic minorities and their white counterparts. Ethnic minority use of these 'White spaces' will support improvements in health and well-being and create the narrative that it is not only middle- and upper-class people who are entitled to clean air . Creating realistic ways for ethnic minorities to access and 'take up space' in what are seen as 'White spaces' could contribute to long-term positive health outcomes and reduce pressures on health services. Public institutions also need to create opportunities for ethnic minorities to enjoy space outside urban environments, facilitated through increased job opportunities and affordable housing as well as information on the risks of poor air quality.

Educate People on How to Fight for Basic Human Rights

Third, it is important to educate people within urban environments about the health dangers of their environments – and what they can do. Teaching people about their human rights and how they can put pressure on governments to make much-needed changes may help to improve the health gap within Britain. A lack of understanding on how to exercise rights leaves citizens unequipped in addressing issues such as air quality. Education systems need to encourage people to utilise their abilities and power to change and impact public policies. The national curriculum should include teaching on the dangers of living in air-polluted environments and go a step further in teaching children and young people how to combat this through action and policy changes. Given the pressures on the NHS due to the health effects of air pollution, the NHS should also invest in creating solutions, supporting preventative measures to improve urban air quality. Educational institutions should work closely with the NHS to educate people in fighting for clean air and promote the benefits that health services would receive if air quality is improved.

GROWING OUR WAY TO HEALTHIER CITIES

Pam Warhurst

During daylight hours in the growing season of many an Incredible Edible town, it's not unusual to see the locals stopping to pick, smell or just have a chat about the food that has been grown to share by other locals of that community – the Incredible Edible volunteers.

Fruit bushes at the doctor's, herbs at the railway station, rhubarb at the college or sweetcorn by the police station.

Such seemingly random behaviour is not the mark of eccentric citizens with time on their hands. It is the purposeful pursuit of a happier, healthier, kinder way of living, open to all, irrespective of age, income, culture or ability.

It is the response of ordinary people to the often overwhelming challenges, amplified by climate change but by no means solely resulting from it, of mental ill-health, obesity particularly among the young, insecurity, poor nutrition and other contemporary health challenges.

The statistics of our population's ill-health have been well rehearsed, as have the financial, social and environmental costs associated with it. Over decades and across continents, the environment we live in, our sense of belonging, the food we eat and the values we share have been demonstrated to be key determinants of public and planetary health. Yet, 27 years and counting after Rio and the first Earth Summit where health was recognised as a marker for a more sustainable future, and 15 years after the Wanless Report, *Securing Good Health for the Whole Population*,[11] we are still apparently in the dark about effectively reducing health inequalities that are a blight on and a cause of shame for twenty-first-century society. At least, through the adoption of the UN Sustainable Development Goals, we now have a means of collectively knowing what good looks like. As for Wanless, we still await a coherent strategy to reduce preventable illness, economic policies which invest in positive health outcomes (such as taxation on junk food) and Cabinet Office health impact assessments of all major policy initiatives – to name just a few.

It was in response to this lack of effective leadership that more than eleven years ago, a bunch of folks in a market town in the north of England decided to roll up their sleeves and in their own small way do something about it, without writing a report, asking permission or waiting for a cheque to drop through the letterbox.

The first question they asked themselves was, How?

How could they, without a bureaucracy behind them, hope to find a mechanism that could enable everyone to understand that they didn't have to see themselves as victims, waiting to be 'done to'; that they had much needed gifts to share and invest in their community; and that they could certainly be a piece of the jigsaw creating a kinder future for their children and for children they may never meet?

I was there at this beginning and it took us all of five minutes to realise the language of opportunity was food. Growing, cooking, buying and sharing. In a multitude of ways food unites us and runs through everything we do. So food became the Trojan Horse of our experiment in tackling some of those wicked issues threatening our well-being.

The second question was, What?

If we were going to start this crazy experiment of volunteers in the place we call home, working at the grassroots, literally, to invest in a healthier, happier, more prosperous society, it would probably be a good idea to have a really simple, shared model to follow.

So we invented our Three Plates model where local food sits centre stage on each one.

Community, Learning and Business reflect three recognisable elements of our everyday experiences.

Our Community Plate focused on the creation of edible landscapes at the heart of our town. From it sprang our propaganda gardens, where unloved pieces of land, often public realm in very public places, became herb gardens, mini orchards or veg plots, always with food to share, created by the community for the community. The idea really took off. We put a call out to plant an orchard on a disused sports pitch and 80 people turned up. We created raised beds at the police station, college and health centre with wood we'd won in a competition and soil donated by a local farmer. We put pots of herbs along the station platform so commuters could help themselves to mint, rosemary or whatever they fancied to go with their evening meal.

Towns from all over the country visited us to see what ideas they could pick up to take back home and become part of the Incredible Edible experiment. Spreading the impact, changing spaces and opening minds. And all we were doing was growing veg.

However, if we were to get more people outdoors, digging their gardens or grass verges or whatever land was available, we had to share a few skills and not just growing ones. Hence our Learning Plate.

People had lost touch with basic cooking skills. Young mums and dads had never peeled a spud, let alone made jam or pickles from excess produce. So, as ever making it up as we went along, we invented the Lost Arts programme where those in our neighbourhoods who had these skills, many of them our older residents, could share what they knew informally, over a cup of tea and a biscuit. We copied a television programme called *Come Dine with Me* to get neighbours sharing food and stories round the kitchen table and we invested in a pop-up tent so we could turn up all over the town, on our estates or right by our local market, demonstrating simple recipes with the stuff growing in the propaganda beds.

People were taking notice. Thinking about food. What grew where and when, and as importantly, what they could do with it. This was just about joining the dots for people, using local food to make connections back in their own kitchens, backyards or gardens.

But we weren't daft. After decades of detachment from the soil and from the skills underpinning putting good fresh food on the table, together with a way of living that wanted everything fast no matter what chemicals and additives were being consumed, we had to help people, particularly the young, to see great local food could be the springboard to a job and maybe the next generation of food entrepreneurs. So, with no budget to call on, we decided to concentrate on our local market hall. After all we were a market town.

We bought six blackboards with our name on the top and gave one to each of the local traders who sold local food. There weren't that many, but there were two butchers, a cheese stall, and a baker. We gave them chalk and asked them to write down anything that was local. It took a while, but after a few months and us promoting it like mad, folks were coming to those stalls and asking about local produce. Sales went up, and soon local cafes were getting the same idea. Small beginnings but the start of an increased interest in local food.

We ran an Every Egg Matters campaign with a map marking places selling local eggs. There were 8 to begin with and 30 by the time we finished. More people taking an interest in local food, and part of a 'sticky money' economy where the profit stays close to the point of production and sale.

All this for one reason. To demonstrate that over time, simply by the way we were living our lives, more and more people were contributing to a new normal. A normal where more folks grew food at home, more folks knew what to do with what they were growing and more people wanted to support their local farmers and other food businesses. Children walking through and by those edible landscapes for the past eleven years stood a better chance of understanding seasonality and where their food came from than those whose only point of reference was a plastic bag of fruit flown half way across the world or pre-packaged ready meals of indeterminate origin.

But this was only ever half the story. As more than a hundred towns, villages and neighbourhoods across the country started to spin their three plates, and many more from New Zealand to Singapore joined our people-powered movement, we recognised that if we were going to have any impact in some of our most disadvantaged areas we had to take the lessons we were all learning about growing and cooking, and challenge those people around board tables who create the frameworks of our lives – local government, the health sector, social landlords and the justice system – to do something different and make it easier for us all to live Incredibly.

So in addition to the amazing network of volunteers creating their propaganda gardens, sharing their growing and cooking skills and working with people of all abilities and circumstances, we gathered the lessons we had learned over a decade of getting on and doing things, and fired them at people we thought could shift the obstacles that stopped many more of us living well and prospering.

We need greater access to more land which we can use to feed ourselves. Investment in an infrastructure that could help us all live well and long. Greater focus on the skills and jobs that could be the bedrock of resourceful communities. Bending existing budgets to move beyond the rhetoric of empowerment, to real enabling through trust in our citizens and belief in the power of small actions.

We put these lessons to everyone from grassroots innovators to institutional influencers, who together could change a variety of systems and open up the possibility of a kinder notion of prosperity.

We were not alone. Brave and prescient local authorities who were wrestling with their ambitions to improve the well-being of their residents in the face of ever-decreasing budgets started to talk to us about how we might work with them to bring about change. Directors of Public Health and Clinical Commissioning Groups were keen to harness the simple and common-sense approach we had demonstrated and help them bring down the numbers of patients in the system through greater physical activity, learning new food skills and reconnecting with good food. People working in the justice system could see the logic of using food skills to build a pathway back out of crime and into the places the offenders called home.

Our asks are eminently achievable.

1. Create an edible public realm.

When local authorities can no longer mow and maintain their public realm, we want to see it become edible, from grass verges, corners of unused brownfield sites through to public parks.

Not exclusively and not everywhere, but to be a much more significant part of the mix.

Public realm is what it says on the label. People's realm, which could be used so much more productively to create healthier living opportunities if people had a greater say in what these spaces were being used for.

2. Plan for food growing in new developments.

With so much attention being given to housebuilding, we want to encourage planners and developers alike to adopt the principles of the Garden City and allocate land around and by new homes to grow food on. Not grassed over rubble or concrete jungles, but food spaces, both formal and informal.

3. Create an Incredible Edible health service.

When it comes to health establishments, our asks are no-brainers. Don't landscape surgeries and hospitals with inedible prickly plants and then run an 'eat five-a-day' campaign. Design all healthcare premises to be significantly edible, so families walking to and from them genuinely begin to see them as pointers to a healthier life rather than the illness centres they are now.

Incorporate community kitchens in or by those health centres, so that patients, community and staff alike can share learning and food, often grown locally, and plan how they might batch-cook for people unable to join them – elderly residents living on their streets, for example.

Challenge health professionals with kindness to use this engagement with growing and cooking food as a social prescribing opportunity.

And as for future skills and jobs, food is the perfect medium for engaging the young in STEAM – science, technology, engineering, arts and maths.

If we are to grow more of our food in our urban centres in decades to come, we'd better start investing in our urban farmers, teaching soil science, hydroponics and aquaponics, producing good food on our doorstep through a variety of techniques. Over and beyond this, we need to inspire our young to be the engineers, architects and planners of the edible settlements of tomorrow, growing food on rooftops and hanging gardens as well as more traditional farms, and designing the infrastructure that is the basis of a local food culture.

All this feels like a new social contract with good food at its heart.

We the people will grow and share food in our communities. We will create more propaganda gardens to inspire interest in local food. We will share the lost arts and we will support local food business.

You, the policymakers and funders, will rethink the use of public realm in partnership with local residents, will make edible landscapes mainstream not just case studies, will invest in infrastructure including community kitchens to give everyone access to the means of producing good food, and when possible, all public institutions will use their procurement budget to support and encourage local supply chains.

This is taking the lessons we have learned from the kitchen table to the boardroom table – joining up the dots for a kinder tomorrow.

Growing this healthier new normal from the grassroots upward can only ever be part of addressing the huge problems of a population's ill-health, but its simplicity, inclusiveness and positivity has meant it has gained traction where other top-down approaches have not.

This is a people-driven approach predicated on trust, hope and the belief in the power of small actions. As Margaret Mead noted, 'Never doubt that a small group of thoughtful, committed citizens can change the world; indeed, it's the only thing that ever has.'

Notes

1. A. Vaughan, 'London's Black Communities Disproportionately Exposed to Air Pollution – Study'. *Guardian*, 10 October 2016. Accessed 18 April 2020. https://www.theguardian.com/environment/2016/oct/10/londons-black-communities-disproportionately-exposed-to-air-pollution-study.
2. *Health Matters: Air Pollution*. Public Health England, 14 November 2018. Accessed 18 April 2020. https://www.gov.uk/government/publications/health-matters-air-pollution/health-matters-air-pollution.
3. Ibid.
4. T. Kjellstrom et al., Urban Environmental Health Hazards and Health Equity', *Journal of Urban Health* 84(3 Supp.) (2007): 86–97. Accessed 18 April 2020. https://www.ncbi.nlm.nih.gov/pubmed/17450427.
5. *Health Matters: Air Pollution*. Public Health England, 14 November 2018. Accessed 18 April 2020. https://www.gov.uk/government/publications/health-matters-air-pollution/health-matters-air-pollution.
6. 'UK's Most Polluted Towns and Cities'. BBC News, 4 May 2018. Accessed 18 April 2020. https://www.bbc.co.uk/news/health-43964341.
7. 'Ella Kissi-Debrah: New Inquest into Girl's "Pollution" Death', BBC News, 2 May 2019. Accessed 18 April 2020. https://www.bbc.co.uk/news/uk-england-london-48132490.
8. R. O'Hare, 'Thousands of Londoners Hospitalised in Three Years Due to Harmful Air Pollution'. Imperial College London, 5 April 2019. Accessed 18 April 2020. https://www.imperial.ac.uk/news/190815/thousands-londoners-hospitalised-three-years-harmful/.
9. *Health Matters: Air Pollution*. Public Health England, 14 November 2018. Accessed 18 April 2020. https://www.gov.uk/government/publications/health-matters-air-pollution/health-matters-air-pollution.
10. B. W. Wheeler and Y. Ben-Shlomo, 'Environmental Equity, Air Quality, Socioeconomic Status, and Respiratory Health: A Linkage Analysis of Routine Data from the Health Survey for England', *Journal of Epidemiology and Community Health* 59 (2005): 948–54. Accessed 18 April 2020. https://jech.bmj.com/content/jech/59/11/948.full.pdf.
11. D. Wanless, 'Securing Good Health for the Whole Population'. HM Treasury, 2004. Accessed 18 April 2020. https://webarchive.nationalarchives.gov.uk/+/http://www.hm-treasury.gov.uk/consult_wanless04_final.htm.

Chapter 7

THE WITHERING CITY

HOW CAN WE SAVE AND RESTORE OUR URBAN GREEN SPACES?

Ian Mell

After ten years of austerity government the United Kingdom's environment is at a tipping point.

Although Defra's 25 Year Environment Plan proposes a set of forward-looking approaches to landscape management, enshrining 'biodiversity net gain' in law on all new development,[1] this is directly countered by the restrictions central government is placing on Local Planning Authorities (LPAs).

Since 2010, LPAs across the United Kingdom have seen cuts in their core budgets of between 20 per cent and 60 per cent, with up to 90 per cent of environment budgets lost in some areas. These 'savings' to central government have hit social, cultural and landscape services hardest. Parks and 'green infrastructure' planning have been disproportionally affected, due to their status as a non-statutory service. In practice this has meant less active management, decreased investment and a rising concern about the deteriorating quality of parks across the United Kingdom, especially in England. This is not the first time this has happened: the 1980s in particular saw systematic cuts in parks funding that decimated public perceptions of parks for a decade. However, we are currently in the most concerted period of funding deficit for a generation.[2] As a consequence, the quality, quantity and longevity of green infrastructure, as a network of local, city and regional landscape elements, are being challenged due to short-sighted financial restructuring.

The UK government's lack of foresight in the way it values the health, well-being, climatic and economic benefits of green and open space is astonishing. By undermining the funding of environmental management, central government increases the risks of flooding, biodiversity decline, and the negative effects of urban heating and air pollution. The shifting of responsibility to the local level, as promoted in the 2011 Localism Act, is also a moral issue.

Central government imposes cuts on LPAs, but refuses to take ownership of the negative effects of these cuts. These have direct costs on individuals and taxpayers, as well as affecting the country's long-term prosperity.

The outcome of these financial choices by government is that our urban areas continue to struggle under austerity. One result is that we can identify real decline in the quality of parks, green spaces and wider green infrastructure networks across our cities.[3] This has direct impacts on the ways in which people access essential green spaces such as local and pocket parks around their homes and workplaces, and engage with the wider countryside, leading to changes in their health and well-being.[4] It also directly limits their opportunities to engage in physical activity or spend time with other people, increasing the risks of social isolation. There is also evidence of direct links between the impacts of poor-quality green infrastructure and reduced well-being as a consequence of climate change, including localised flooding, temperature fluctuations and changes in air quality. Growing concerns about air pollution around schools in London have led to proposals for green infrastructure as a solution to an emerging public health emergency. However, in areas of socio-economic and democratic inequality, including inner-city areas and some rural communities, we can see dramatic variations in the funding and types of green spaces available to people. Assessments undertaken in Sheffield, London and Glasgow suggest that people in areas where employment, educational standards, affluence and health are worse are being disproportionally harmed by austerity and its impacts on the physical environment. Furthermore, such locations are more likely to have poor-quality parks and poorly maintained green spaces with limited functionality. Arguably, government policy is hurting those in greatest need. If you're poor in the United Kingdom you are more likely to experience climate poverty and live in an area of poor-quality public and green space, exacerbating any other socio-economic problems you may face.

People in the United Kingdom are therefore being placed in a precarious position socioculturally and environmentally, and many communities are unable to address the problems forced upon them. However, there is also a growing realisation, especially in Scotland and Wales, that the environment, and specifically the *local environment*, is worth fighting for. This can include reactions to transport infrastructure, including the proposed expansions of Manchester and Heathrow airports, the felling of healthy street trees in Sheffield, the conversion of green spaces or parklands in Liverpool to luxury homes and calls to address the lack of access to green space linked to historical health inequality in central Scotland.

Within each of these locations the public and landscape, health and planning professionals are willing to give their time, experience and knowledge, and in some cases their freedom, to stand up for nature. Each example illustrates the passion local people feel and value they attribute to local green infrastructure in improving their lives and their communities. The public have also acted as a moral barometer for local and central government, highlighting the damaging and unwelcome character of the conversion, sale or reduced maintenance of local green spaces.[5]

To address the systematic changes in local government financing for the environment a growing number of organisations have stepped forward to illustrate alternative approaches. These include the use of the Green Space Factor in the City of London, which requires all new development to invest in on-site greening to gain planning approval,[6] the continued enthusiasm for guerrilla gardening and use of temporary spaces through projects such as Incredible Edible, the rise in local doctors prescribing green exercise programmes in Glasgow, and the interest in asset transfers of parks and open spaces to local communities. Each shows how financing, time and capacity can be found to meet local landscape needs. However, they are not a panacea for the ills of austerity. It is therefore imperative that we look more deeply at the programmes, projects and people who are leading the search for tenable and transferable solutions.

Austerity has energised the responses of the public in the United Kingdom, and internationally, to landscape decline. Across the United Kingdom, campaign groups are fighting to protect parks, green spaces, water quality and access to public space, as they view these amenities as (a) a right; (b) as essential to their quality of life; and (c) valuable to the quality of the urban environment. In Liverpool the Save Newsham Park, Walton Hall Park and Sefton Park Meadows campaigns have encouraged Liverpool City Council to rethink its stance on the sale or conversion of parkland into housing. These groups have fostered a sense of community empowerment that has had a tangible influence on how the city undertakes development. This reinforces the value of social protest in challenging government mandates, as seen historically in the National Parks and Access to the Countryside Act (1949), Countryside and Rights of Way Act (2000) and the designation and retention of Green Belts from 1955 onwards. This shows the appetite within local communities to fight for the environment. The retention of our parks and green infrastructure is the latest articulation of this resistance to enforced environmental damage.

One way to move forward from public protest has been to transfer public assets into community hands. Projects such as Heeley Park in Sheffield illustrate how an informed and entrepreneurial approach to park management can be aligned with hard work and community commitment to create and maintain essential local green spaces.[7] Using a mixed approach to funding, the Heeley Park management team have diversified the organisation's approach to financing, enabling them to apply for and obtain financial support from a range of funders. This has placed them outside the direct line of LPA and central government funding in many instances, providing the park with a more robust and sustainable base for ongoing management. Although Heeley Park is not representative of all communities or their ability to take ownership of local parks, it does illustrate the potential local groups have to take a much greater role in managing local spaces.

There is also a growing discussion on how to encourage private businesses to put something back into the communities they reside in. Through Corporate Social Responsibility (CSR) programmes some companies are working to ensure that they do not simply 'take' from the local environment. They are using greener campuses and workplaces, environmental volunteering and capital investment in urban greening to promote awareness of the environmental value of green infrastructure within commercial activities.[8] They can go further though: there is scope for greater encouragement, coercion or collaboration between private and civic organisations to invest in and manage green and open spaces. There is a role for businesses through Business Improvement Districts (BIDs), Local Enterprise Partnerships (LEPs), the NHS and police/fire services, major sports clubs/facilities, and universities who all have the potential, and in many cases a 'civic duty', to lead this change, and deliver more effective environmental management in urban areas.

These examples illustrate that we do not need to simply follow existing practices but can, and should, be innovative in funding landscape resources. Through the invigoration created by entrepreneurial advocates there is scope to find solutions to the problems created by central government. It also highlights that individuals, communities and organisations are willing to step into the breach and fight for the environment in ways that may have previously been marginalised or isolated. However, the fight is not over, and securing long-term financial stability for investment in green and open spaces remains fragile.

So, what can we do?

The following three proposals set out a call to arms for LPAs, communities, and the public and private sectors to create a sustainable legacy for environmental management in the United Kingdom, and internationally:

1. Reverse all funding cuts for green and open spaces and restore LPAs' financial stability and their ability to spend on landscape projects.
2. Make environmental education and championing a parameter of all public sector work/funding, and legislate to move private business into more ecologically sustainable practices.

3. Legislate for green infrastructure to be required in all new and retrofitted development, and allow LPAs to pursue legal means to challenge developers who attempt to dodge their environmental responsibilities.

To achieve these ambitious objectives, the following more detailed processes should be followed.

First, to address the negative impacts of austerity on people, the environment and society, funding for green infrastructure needs to be restored to at least pre-2010 levels. This needs to go beyond simply reversing the cuts, as the situation has changed dramatically since the Conservative–Liberal Democrat Coalition and subsequent Conservative governments took office. The embedding of biodiversity net gain in the 2019 Environment Bill is one way to ensure financial support is provided for green infrastructure, but more is needed to ensure LPAs have the capacity to create and manage attractive and multifunctional landscapes. Above-inflation investment in urban landscapes is therefore critical to the ongoing functionality of our cities.

Second, a nationwide programme of awareness raising supported or managed by the NHS, UK government, Natural England, civic and private institutions, and other notable environmental champions such as the National Trust, should be rolled out to promote an understanding of the value of green infrastructure to all. This could be achieved via primary and secondary school programmes, as well as being embedded in adult and elderly care. Opportunities also exist to integrate landscape management and maintenance into employability programmes (e.g. as part of jobseeking schemes). Yes, this will cost money, but the payback in terms of long-term environmental resilience and the reduction of deaths from air pollution, for example, makes the cost–benefit analysis positive for investment in environmental education.

Third, green infrastructure and its funding should be required by law in all medical, schooling, business and economic development briefs. It should be a legal requirement that all development should (a) provide new/enhanced green infrastructure, (b) promote access to neighbourhood and larger green sites and (c) promote biodiversity net gain (on and off-site). Some LPAs already have precepts on local taxes to pay for green infrastructure, such as around Epping Forest, so rolling out a precept charge to fund parks and open spaces in all areas is not beyond planning authorities' legal capacity. It may be unpopular with people who don't use green infrastructure, but would provide ring-fenced funding to ensure the environment is maintained. Moreover, LPAs could be given the *actual* power to enforce planning obligations and collect development contributions in the form of S106 and Community Infrastructure Levy (CIL) payments through legal recourse. This would face challenges from developers regarding the 'viability' of investment, but such a shift is needed.

Finally, central government needs to be accountable for the societal problems it has created. It needs to acknowledge its impacts on the social and physical landscape of the United Kingdom and find deliverable solutions to these issues. Platitudes are not good enough anymore. Action is needed now to repair the negativity people feel due to austerity, and only through drastic changes in funding will the landscape of the United Kingdom maintain its aesthetic and functional value.

CITIES CAN BE GREEN HAVENS

Natalie Bennett

Despite the reputation of the United Kingdom as a nation of animal lovers, it is one of the most nature-depleted nations on the globe and there has been no let-up in the loss of nature in the United Kingdom, as revealed by the 2019 State of Nature Report.[9] The focus on the immediate causes of recent decades of major decline is, rightly, on farming practices and climate change. However, little attention has been given to the potential for urban design, planning and management to make a real impact, for good or ill.

A lot of attention has been directed to the fate of bees and other pollinators, which, with many other groups, are suffering serious declines. But these crucial species provide an important pointer to this planning perspective: urban bees are doing better than rural, benefiting from the relative biodiversity of cities, compared with the large-scale industrial monoculture and blanketed herbicides and pesticides of rural areas.

Cities can be green havens. They can compete with even a rejuvenated countryside for maximum benefit to nature and people, making sure corridors are planned and provided so species can move through them, making the most of canals and parks, planting native species, encouraging insects.

The focus on biodiversity and bioabundance among the species we see around us (or all too often note their absence) is a welcome new side to our debate about the public realm of our cities. Tackling the sterilisation of the countryside – the hideous slaughter on the grouse moors, the blanketing of rapeseed crops in fungicides, the dumping of metaldehyde on our land – are issues for another place, but a concern for nature and its promotion can be and is very much a part of our urban communities.

A whole new developing field of research is adding weight to the support for plants and animals, recognising the importance of the microbial life that accompany them, the bacteria and fungi that we are increasingly coming to realise are crucial to our health and well-being – as well as that of the many other species with which we share our cities. That's won the United Nations' attention in the form of the Healthy Urban Microbiome Initiative (HUMI),[10] recognising that 'high quality, biodiverse green spaces in our cities [...] maximise population health benefits, bring significant savings to health budgets, while delivering gains for biodiversity'.

Meanwhile so many of the natural environments in the cities of the United Kingdom are suffering further degradation, rather than the investment and support they so desperately need. Austerity programmes and 'selling off the family silver' have seen government bodies at all levels desperately trying to monetise any assets they can sell – from school playing fields to corners of land of NHS hospitals – or renting them out to raise funds (essential city green spaces designed for the public are being rented out for private events), or reducing staffing on maintenance and clean-up.

On private land we're seeing far too much concreting over, a destruction of bioabundance that's linked to the continued dominance of the private motor vehicle in our cities. In London this dominance results in the loss of green garden space equivalent to the area of Hyde Park every year. The discussion about that has tended to focus on the flooding impacts, but they clearly also cause a significant loss of plants and space for animals.[11]

The expansion of private rented housing is a further factor, very evident in cities like my own, Sheffield. Private rented accommodation, particularly for students, and short-term, lower-cost, often very poor-quality, accommodation, is identifiable by the concreting over of yards and the removal of every possible natural feature such as a tree or shrub that might require some maintenance or attention.

Focusing on the damage done by Westminster austerity, while accurate, is far from the whole story. We don't want to go back to 2010, or even earlier, to some sort of 'green' age – it was nothing of the sort. The whole approach to urban environments, and large amounts of investment, was built on the idea of 'tidiness'. Swathes of grass were to be maintained, regularly trimmed and any 'weeds' (for which hear wildflowers) ruthlessly exterminated with toxic herbicides. Trees were tightly regulated, fruiting species grubbed out because they 'make a mess', and garden beds regularly replanted with monocultures of pansies or primulas, species with few environmental benefits.

Visitors were to be kept off the grass, children chased down from any tree they might venture to climb and insects were generally seen as pests to be controlled, not crucial foundations of the ecosystem. Birds were to be chased from any inconvenient nesting site.

Since then we have seen some progress, although considerably less in the United Kingdom than in other parts of Europe. The idea of not regularly mowing at least some verges, but instead managing them for wildflowers, particularly those of benefit to pollinators, has taken at least tentative hold, from Green stronghold Stroud, where I've stood in the middle of wonderfully colourful swathes humming with insects, to pioneering Rotherham in the north. In this area at least, there's a sign of austerity having a rare positive impact.

Environmental charity Plantlife, with other charities, has just reported on how sensible, cheaper, management of verges could provide Britain with 400 billion more wildflowers, on spaces that – with 97 per cent of meadows lost – are a crucial refuge, home to 45 per cent of Britain's flora species.[12] Community action has also played its part in guerrilla gardening and sometimes the more formal creation of pocket parks, small spaces often in tightly built-up areas.

Spreading knowledge of the collapse of the hedgehog population, and understanding that fragmented habitat is probably its biggest problem, has led to modest schemes to provide small gaps in fences to allow them to roam over new suburban estates.[13] I've yet to see a substantial housing scheme planted for maximum wildlife benefit, however.

In Sheffield in 2018, I saw a small example of how far we have to go in our attitude to managing existing spaces. Opposite my house is a doctor's surgery with a car park. A corner of that had been planted with a few small trees, but over perhaps a dozen years nature had done its stuff, and the lollipop trees had been surrounded by self-seeded buddleia and rowans, with an understorey of mixed shrubs, home to a small flock of sparrows, a few tits and a family of blackbirds, humming with bees in summer.

One morning I woke to find contractors at work, felling the lot. The next week I went into the doctor's surgery and got a confused explanation, about preventing litter, about some possible future building extension (for which no planning application has been made) and the desire for tidiness. It's now a litter-strewn mess, the car park is exposed in all its unattractive greyness, and impossible to say if those displaced birds found a new mid-winter home. The city is the poorer, for nature and people.[14]

There's still a strong inclination that when the money can be found, nature needs to be 'tidied up', rather than encouraged and nurtured as though our future depended on it, which of course it does. Buckinghamshire County Council is right at the top of pyramid of shame with this approach, having proudly declared at the start of 2019 that despite austerity, it had found half a million pounds to tidy up 'unwanted greenery' in its towns and villages, promising three applications of herbicide (probably glyphosate) to ensure no bit of nature is left to survive.[15]

I write this from Sheffield, a city now infamous for the council's tree-felling policies, that saw thousands of healthy trees felled under the saws of private contractor Amey with a 25-year street management contract aimed at avoiding maintenance costs. The council was signatory to a contract that demanded 'tidiness', straight kerbs and standard-size kerbstones that cut a swathe through the bioabundance of significant areas (as well as destroying a great deal of beauty).

The positive to come from that has been a new focus on the value of street trees far beyond Yorkshire. I was particularly delighted to see a social media post from New Delhi speaking of this fight as an inspiration. People power has finally secured most of the remaining threatened trees in Sheffield. Another sign of progress.

But when I visit new housing estates (and offices) in Sheffield and beyond, I cannot but reflect on how far we have to go, and what our cities could be as a haven for nature – and a healthy environment for us all. They're still far too often built for the car, with acres of hardstanding and barely a plant in sight. Fruit trees or bushes – like the maintenance-free gooseberry bush in my back garden that this summer filled my freezer – are a totally foreign concept, even though they should be an obvious feature, of benefits to humans and wildlife.

Of course that's true of our Victorian terraced streets too, packed with cars so densely that buses and emergency vehicles frequently struggle to get through. Scant space for nature or fruit or other trees on these – just the hunks of metal and rubber that spend well over 90 per cent of their time unused, stationary, wasting space that could be available to people and nature.

I've seen in the centre of historic Ghent just the germ of a change in how our cities could be. With cars essentially banished, roads are reclaimed for bicycles, for playgrounds, even for plantings. It is a start. Our fast-emptying out-of-town shopping centres, with their acres of empty Tarmac, can also be put to good use, as I was musing way back in 2006 after my first Green Party conference.[16]

We've also got a long way to go to think about how our cities are hostile environments for animals and people in less physically tangible ways. Awareness of the damage of light and noise pollution – both to birds and people – has just started to land. It will be interesting to see any impacts from France, where the use of neon shop signs has recently been banned from midnight until dawn. The reason was saving power, thinking of our climate emergency, but there will surely be benefits for wildlife.

We're just starting to acknowledge the damage done by noise, particularly from vehicles (and aircraft). There's also the beginnings of an understanding of how wildlife struggle also – with many songbirds singing louder and higher than their country cousins, which can hardly be good for their well-being.

Nitrates are another rising area of concern, with urban waterways affected too by the rising temperatures of the climate emergency, the runoff from garden fertiliser and possibly also uncollected domestic animal faeces. Choking algal blooms, sometimes poisonous, are not the kind of urban flowering we want to see.

How much better if we find ways to recycle those nutrients – including those produced by people – for fertilising plants, and often plants for food. Sustainable Urban Drainage Schemes – still far too often reserved for award-winning 'blue-ribbon' sites – can capture not just water but also nutrients, and use them rather than treat them as pollutants.

Incredible Edible, starting in Todmorden, has spread its doctrine of urban food-growing in pretty well any space at all. I loved the maize in the police station yard with the 'don't pick (until a couple more weeks when it is ripe)' sign.

Such food-growing, particularly if incorporating permaculture principles, has the potential to be a refuge and haven for wildlife, microflora and microfauna, and the supplies can help to replace those from countryside areas being rewilded for nature and carbon storage benefits.

All of these suggestions for nature are often dismissed as unrealistic, costly or 'difficult'. But as the phrase goes, there is no alternative. We have to stem and reverse the collapse of the biodiversity that our lives depend on.

The changes proposed would also make our communities far more liveable, far more healthy places for human beings – a reminder that we also are part of nature, and cannot divorce ourselves from its complex, messy, untidy realities. And it is not as if what we are doing with most of our urban planning now has much to recommend it for our wellbeing, or our future.

So what is to be done?

1. Local authorities and road authorities need to focus their own land management on maximising biodiversity and bioabundance, ensuring that it is only damaged when absolutely necessary, and boosted whenever possible. Landowners and managers must act in the same manner. The law must be changed to prevent land use that imposes externalised costs on others, including loss of biodiversity and bioabundance.
2. Planning laws should make preserving and enhancing biodiversity and bioabundance an obligation. No hard landscaping unless absolutely essential, and green roofs, tree-planting, landscaping to maximise biodiversity and bioabundance.
3. As well as promoting active transport (walking and cycling) and public transport (including free buses), plus widespread provision of car clubs, local authorities should open up the street and public parking spaces freed up to community uses – playgrounds, food-growing, tree-planting, community socialising.

Notes

1 *A Green Future: Our 25 Year Plan to Improve the Environment*. HM Government, 2018. Accessed 18 April 2020. https://assets.publishing.service.gov.uk/government/uploads/system/uploads/attachment_data/file/693158/25-year-environment-plan.pdf.
2 Nesta, *Learning to Rethink Parks* (London: Nesta, 2016).
3 P. Neal, *Rethinking Parks: Exploring New Business Models for Parks in the 21st Century*. Nesta, 2013. Accessed 18 April 2020. https://www.nesta.org.uk/report/rethinking-parks-new-business-models-for-parks/.
4 I. Mell, 'National Parks Are Beautiful, but Austerity and Inequality Prevent Many from Enjoying Them'. *Conversation*, 20 February 2019. Accessed 18 April 2020. https://theconversation.com/national-parks-are-beautiful-but-austerity-and-inequality-prevent-many-from-enjoying-them-111768.
5 I. Mell, 'Financing the Future of Green Infrastructure Planning: Alternatives and Opportunities in the UK', *Landscape Research* 43(6) (2018): 751–68. Accessed 18 April 2020. https://doi.org/10.1080/01426397.2017.1390079.

6. Mayor of London, *The London Plan – The Spatial Development Strategy for London Consolidated with Alterations since 2011*. Mayor of London, 2016. Accessed 18 April 2020. https://www.london.gov.uk/sites/default/files/the_london_plan_2016_jan_2017_fix.pdf.
7. 'Heeley Development Trust: Heeley Subscription Society'. Nesta. Accessed 24 October 2019. Accessed 18 April 2020. https://www.nesta.org.uk/project/rethinking-parks/heeley-subscription-society/.
8. Grosvenor, *Living Cities: Our Approach in Practice* (London: Grosvenor, 2015).
9. National Trust and Others, *State of Nature 2019*. Accessed 18 April 2020. https://nbn.org.uk/wp-content/uploads/2019/09/State-of-Nature-2019-UK-full-report.pdf.
10. Healthy Urban Microbiome Initiative. Accessed 24 October 2019. https://www.humi.site.
11. Royal Horticultural Society, *Greening Grey Britain*. RHS, 2016. Accessed 18 April 2020. https://www.rhs.org.uk/communities/archive/PDF/Greener-Streets/greening-grey-britain-report.pdf.
12. 'Managing Grassland Road Verges'. Plantlife. Accessed 4 October 2019. https://www.plantlife.org.uk/uk/our-work/publications/road-verge-management-guide.
13. 'Hedgehogs and Development'. British Hedgehog Preservation Society. Accessed 14 October 2019.
    https://www.britishhedgehogs.org.uk/wp-content/uploads/2019/05/developers-1.pdf.
14. N. Bennett, 'We Need a War on Tidiness'. *Ecologist*, 1 March 2019. Accessed 18 April 2020. https://theecologist.org/2019/mar/01/we-need-war-tidiness.
15. J. Rapson, 'Extra £500,000 to Be Spent on Killing Weeds in "Scruffy" Towns and Villages'. *Bucks Free Press*, 11 February 2019. Accessed 18 April 2020. https://www.bucksfreepress.co.uk/news/17424434.bucks-county-council-allocates-extra-500000-on-killing-weeds-in-scruffy-towns-and-villages/.
16. N. Bennett, 'Making the Tarmac Bloom'. *Guardian*, 25 September 2006. Accessed 18 April 2020. https://www.theguardian.com/commentisfree/2006/sep/25/makingthetarmacbloom.

Chapter 8

THE DISPOSSESSED CITY

DISPOSSESSION THROUGH GENTRIFICATION

Loretta Lees

Dispossessed – displaced, un-homed, uprooted, evicted, ousted, rejected, divested, expelled, cast out, expropriated – the negative outcome of gentrification.

Urban dispossession is occurring worldwide in the name of progress, modernisation, regeneration and revitalisation. In the global South increasing numbers of poor people are being forced from their homes to allow for urban redevelopment projects, through the use of violence, intimidation or coercion. But in the Global North, and in the United Kingdom, we are also seeing heightened examples of this kind of urban crisis. This can be seen in growing housing insecurity, new forms of social inequality, and household displacement, much of it from gentrification. State-led gentrification is taking place more often than not on formerly public land. In this contribution I focus on London, a city in which intensifying forms of gentrification are causing multiple, variegated dispossessions. The dispossessed city points to a crisis in urban land ownership; here I focus specifically on public land and the council housing on it.

The State-Led Gentrification of Council Estates in London

Organic 'gentrification' that began in the United Kingdom in the mid-1960s has been increasingly overtaken by accelerated forms in which the state is often a key player, taking on an important role in remaking and gentrifying the city. From 2008, government austerity measures have massively affected local authority revenues, and London councils, like many others across the United Kingdom, have turned to making money from the sale of the public land on their books. This has been aided by council estates being designated as 'brownfield sites' to be redeveloped – usually as mixed-income city 'villages'. The Mayor of London's 2014 Housing Strategy called for the 'vast development potential in London's existing affordable housing estates' to be unlocked through private redevelopment. To 'kick-start and accelerate' that process, the government launched a £150-million Estate Regeneration Programme of loans to private developers 'redeveloping existing estates' on 'a mixed tenure basis', in so doing continuing New Labour's mixed communities policy which had already been identified by some as a kind of 'gentrification by stealth'.

Income from planning gain (the additional public benefits gained from developers during the granting of planning permission) is supposedly enabling local councils to pay (in a time of severe cuts) for housing, roads, social services and so on. Indeed, many local authorities have been lobbying central government to make planning gain a central plank of national planning policy. The oft-cited narrative of developers taking all, or most, of the profit does not always capture what are, in practice, often muddier processes. Some local authorities in London have tried to control developers' benefits and profits, but the picture is complex and in some cases authorities have insufficiently reined-in profit motives or plans that have given little in return to existing communities. Local decisions are not all the same, but in many respects the outcomes are remarkably similar – the gentrification of council estate communities and movement towards a doughnut city model of wealthy elites at the centre and the poor pushed out to the periphery.

In 2015, the London Assembly estimated that, between 1994 and 2004, 50 former council estates across London had received planning permission for partial or complete demolition and redevelopment at higher densities. Recent research[1] has found 198 regeneration schemes since 1997, affecting 161 council estates across London, with approximately 150,000 council estate residents being affected by decanting (residents being moved out as a precursor to development). These estates have been/are being subject to significant demolition and the subsequent densification or intensification of land use. These are just the figures for London. Similar processes are emerging in other UK cities, if at a smaller scale.

Council estates have long been seen as protecting low-income groups from the high cost of private housing and the takeover of sections of the city by capital and the middle classes in the form of gentrification, especially in inner London. But this role is quickly evaporating and is being mirrored in cities such as Manchester, Leeds and Glasgow (take a look at the demolition threat to the close-knit council estate community of Oulton in Leeds). Council estate residents are under threat of what I have called 'accumulative dispossession' from numerous sources. This includes the demolition of council estates but also results from the impact of austerity measures (including housing benefit changes), and the rise of precarity in the labour market through, for example, zero-hour contracts, which results in many tenants struggling to pay their rent and bills. Both people and places, including local neighbourhoods in many

UK cities, but also almost entire cities like London, are becoming more precarious and socially homogenous as a result.

The planned, deliberate destruction of council estate residents' homes causes emotional trauma: anxiety, confusion, fear, dislocation, loss, dread, stress, depression and even suicide or early death. Here is an example, an account by a council tenant going through these processes first-hand:

> I had friends down there and they all moved outside of London to different places. And they asked me if I wanted to move outside of London, and I said 'No thanks.' I will stay where I am, I have got the family around, although they annoy me half of the time [...] they are my family, and I appreciate their being around. Now if I was to move outside of London and that, within three months, I would be dead!

The lack of control over being decanted and the difficulty of finding a replacement home is often described as 'living on a knife edge'. The violence of dispossession can be fast or slow and the speed causes different psychological and social responses. When the speed is slow and percolating, tenants' mental health is impacted on a daily basis by years of living with uncertainty, as estate 'regeneration' slowly unwinds, as this council tenant under threat of displacement describes:

> It is awful, and it is something, because of the uncertainty, all of those years you have been living with uncertainty. On top, if you have the mental health issues, I end up having most of the night, having a nightmare. And, all of the night I have been seeing, looking for a home but not finding a home. And then waking up really, sometimes, my sister wakes me up, because of my shouting. And everything, and you still have to put a mask on your face, and go out and fight for your community, fight for your home.

Critically the security of home, even for those who bought their council home through right to buy as a way to increase their lived and financial security, is destroyed, as this interview with a leaseholder being displaced from an estate in London describes:

> It's with retrospect [...] I'd bought it (her flat) as a security [...] I was in a most insecure position and not knowing how to get out of the situation I was in. [...] Not so much trapped, as [...] I failed everything [...] I was approaching 60 and hadn't managed to look after myself. Then it just snowballed into this. It was like every decision you had made in your life was wrong. I think you're just

feeling like you haven't made a success of your life, you can't afford to look after yourself, and just the accumulation. It didn't matter what I did. I mean I know everything is about perspective. It's trying to change my perspective on things and work out what to do and I couldn't work out anything. Everything I was told was just a lie that I'd be looked after and secure.

There is little or no scope within existing policies of regeneration to recognise that the goal of improving these areas is, in reality, highly damaging to individuals and communities. Worse, these forms of displacement are a breach of human rights and create social and economic disbenefits, doing nothing for the social well-being of either them or the area they live/d in.[2]

An Agenda for Action

I am always being asked at public events: how do we stop gentrification? I always struggle to reply, for of course the probability of being able to overturn global capitalism is not good! But a focus on the role of the state gives hope here, for there is some possibility of stopping state-led gentrification and influencing how the state acts in the future.

The three concrete, ambitious but achievable ideas that I would like to happen in the very near future are the following:

1. New laws to retain public land in England for public use and the common good in perpetuity.
2. National policy that both retains but also builds more council homes.
3. National policy supporting Community Land Trusts (CLTs) legally and financially.

These ideas are underpinned by protecting public land before it is all sold off; protecting and building the only truly affordable housing that most people need – council housing (recognising that UK housing associations have become mini property developers and social cleansers in their own right – most recently in central Rochdale, where College Bank is under threat of demolition with tower blocks redeveloped as townhouses); and a commitment to decommodifying housing by supporting and scaling up CLTs (which to date have been small and niche) to eliminate speculative investment by the propertied elite. This would mean a turn away from the privatisation of council housing for the poor, taking it back into municipal control and/or turning it over to CLTs to be run by local communities.

The first idea can gain real traction from recent discussions about a 'new' municipal socialism and new models of governance and community wealth building. Maintaining the freehold of land in public ownership would protect council estates against privatisation, and retain public land for council house building, allowing councils to generate an income stream over time. In addition, public land could be given over to, or leased to, CLTs that could help local councils whose economic power has been reduced due to austerity, support the local economy, and support local democracy and community building.

The second idea is already being mooted by both the Greens and Labour (albeit many Labour-run boroughs are still going ahead with estate demolitions) but we need to strategise better on this: developing properly evidenced proposals on finance models for new council housing and the refurbishment of estates under threat of demolition (keeping residents in place). There needs to be proper policy discussion on the gentrification caused by mixed communities policy in the United Kingdom and a rejection or revision of this policy. Here the state needs to be given an ambitious role at the forefront of actions and solutions. John Healey, Labour's former housing spokesperson, announced plans in 2018 for a new English Sovereign Land Trust to buy land at a price closer to its actual value rather than its potential value. Such a move would require a change to the 1961 Land Compensation Act, but it would also enable the construction of council housing more cheaply and could help in the fight against gentrification which often takes place as an exploitation of this rent gap. Beyond this any response to the contemporary urban crisis needs to address the question of who owns urban land, what is done with it and how these factors address or undermine the needs of urban communities.

The third idea, CLTs, have long been seen as an alternative to gentrification. They allow us to work around the dominance of profit motives by taking property and land out of the market. In CLTs a community organisation owns and manages the land, and the residents own only the housing units located on the land. There are strict limits on housing costs and the resale price of units, and people can only collect on investments they make in the units – for any rise in housing value is socially created and not something that belongs to any individual. Land and buildings are separated so that any uplift in value is retained in perpetuity by the community. CLTs establish new kinds of social environments in which it is 'normal' to know your neighbours (doing the social mixing that mixed communities policy desires) and to contribute to the upkeep of the neighbourhood.[3]

Jess Steele OBE, a community activist who has first-hand experience of setting up CLTs in the United Kingdom (see her contribution in Chapter 10), argues strongly why, but also how, they can be an achievable alternative to gentrification. She puts on the table a 'coordinated action to create a cross-class, difference-embracing, open, collaborative process in good faith to self-renovate, to make our own neighbourhoods better for us and for others without that being a class-driven aspiration'[4]. Such a programme, she argues, would 'require social ownership of housing, social production of housing supply, public control of housing finance capital, social control of land, resident control of neighbourhoods, affirmative action and housing choice, and equitable resource allocation'. Rather than profit underlying decisions about housing, they would focus instead on socially determined need. There does, however, need to be much more discussion on new models of (self)governance with respect to community control.

On top of these 'protections' for low-income groups, I would like to see reformed national taxation of property that takes into account actual values and new legislation on land value capture that enables local communities to recover and reinvest land value increases for public benefit. We need a thorough rethink of Amin, Massey and Thrift's *Cities for the Many, Not the Few*,[5] which has been criticised for being liberal rather than radical, ignoring questions of marginality, and feeding into New Labour's urban renaissance agenda that supported the destruction of council estates and, ironically, resulted in cities for the few, not the many. We need to take seriously the idea that properly affordable housing (and affordable housing is not 80 per cent market rate) is a human right. We need to build new forms of personal and local housing security. Indeed, twenty years later, what might a new version of that book look like?

LAND AND DISPLACEMENT

Kate Swade and Mark Walton

The way land is invested in, managed and owned in our towns and cities is a key element of the 'urban crisis'. A significant part of this crisis has been generated by a shift in ownership from public to private and its effect in squeezing out space for leisure, living, political and personal forms of expression. These are not new issues, but they have certainly become more visible as living spaces get smaller and space outside the home is increasingly privatised. The effect of these changes has been to create more constrained and commodified spaces as we lose more and more of the places where we might otherwise gather freely, express ourselves and make some kind of mark – physical or cultural – upon the fabric of the places where we live.

Land is fundamentally different to any forms of property. No one has made it, and supply cannot be increased in response to increased demand. This is especially so in urban areas, where land is given its 'value' – the price the landowner wants for it – by its location, and the actions of the state and the community surrounding it, including public investments in infrastructure, private investment in business and neighbouring properties, as well as the rules and frameworks contained in our planning system. Land accounts for 51 per cent of the United Kingdom's net worth, according to the Office for National Statistics.

These values vary according to particular city context. London is a hotbed of high land values, with the gap in average house prices between London and the rest of the country growing wider nearly every year since 1995.[6] These high prices (and the promise of continued growth) result in increasing land values and the development of ever-higher and more dense new buildings, designed to recoup the high cost of land but also to maximise profits, often sacrificing good design or contribution to community life in the process. The herd of cranes looming over London's skyline tells the story of multiple 'unique landmark developments', each representing a sizeable rock thrown into the pond of the local social ecosystems around them. While each locality is unique, the ripples from these pebbles look similar in many places – rents rise, local people and institutions are displaced, local businesses lose out to chain stores better able to pay increasing rents on ever bigger units.

Cities with lower land values suffer from different symptoms, often arising from the same basic underlying cause. Land may be abandoned if industry and capital withdraw, close or relocate. This kind of disinvestment may lead to empty shops and struggling high streets, with householders facing negative equity as the value of their home falls, while landowners wait for the tide of capital investment to turn and for prices to rise. These different, market-driven situations have been compounded by austerity and systemic disinvestment in public services. This has taken the form of cuts to vital individual services like youth services, children's services and adult social care, but also to crucial common provision that includes parks, libraries and support for the voluntary sector. These cuts squeeze the space for common and community life out of our cities, and constrain the space for non-commercial activities as land and buildings are sold off to generate capital receipts and the remaining assets are commercialised to generate ongoing revenue. Since 1980 half of all public land in the United Kingdom has been sold off – 10 per cent of the entire land mass.[7]

These losses are rarely regained or offset by the creation of new green spaces and community assets, such as those provided in some new housing developments. Developers have a set formula to appraise potential developments, which includes the aspiration for 20 per cent profit. If this can't be achieved the scheme is considered to be 'unviable'. Viability gets used as an excuse for not providing new green spaces and community facilities in both high and low land value scenarios. In high land value areas the argument is often that the land cost too much in the first place to allow for the provision of non-profit-making space. Conversely, in low land value areas, the viability calculation is based on lower sales values rather than higher prices, which has a similar effect in terms of arguing down contribution to public space.

Where new green spaces and community facilities are created, local authorities rarely take on the ownership and management roles they once did. Instead, the developer will often put in place a private management arrangement, paid for by residents through a service charge or maintenance fee. In many cases residents find themselves paying for services with no control over their price, the quality delivered, or the rules that dictate who may use the space or what they may do there. Not only are the spaces themselves being privatised but so is their long-term management, paid for by residents even though it is not accountable to them. As a result apparently 'public' spaces are increasingly privately owned and managed, and subject to rules that make them more manageable for the owner rather than as spaces for social connection, individual reflection and expression, or collective political action – with all the messiness and unpredictability that these activities imply. As Churchill foresaw, much of this crisis has arisen through the way in which we treat land as a commodity rather than a public good.

Disconnecting the City

This commodification of land results in a lack of connection and belonging, creating instead a set of transactional relationships between individuals and the spaces they inhabit. The reducing role of the state increasingly means that the economy is owned and run by organisations far away from communities, and decisions are made based on commercial considerations by people who often have no connection to a local area or accountability to those that live there.

As work becomes ever more precarious, and the money we spend on housing, travel and leisure and entertainment increases, we also see a corresponding pressure to deliver cheaper food and other commodities.[8] This creates knock-on impacts that ripple out from cities to the countryside and onwards into a global food system that undervalues growers, driving rural precarity and an unsustainable focus on yields and efficiency in agriculture at the expense of our soils and environment. Amid this precarity we are increasingly exhorted by politicians to volunteer to keep local parks, libraries, community facilities and even pubs and shops operating. Capital is always keen to embrace free labour and contribution to maintain high profit rates. Yet, while volunteering can be a valuable way of building social connections and creating a sense of belonging, this new type of civic action is often focused on maintaining valued assets and services endangered by the withdrawal of the state, rather than as an expression of genuine agency or belonging.

While the opportunities for people to become 'placekeepers' and take some control over aspects of their local areas are increasing, their ability to do so is often dependent on their existing resources of time, money, knowledge and connections. Those who already have some degree of security are much more able to secure the future of the land and buildings that matter to them than those who are already running to stand still, or who have already suffered years of neglect, disinvestment, dispossession or marginalisation.

Building the Common Good

In our organisation, Shared Assets, we have started addressing these issues from the belief that land is a common good that should be managed in ways that provide shared benefits, not just private gain irrespective of who owns it. We have worked with community organisations, public and private landowners, researchers, academics and entrepreneurs to develop new models of environmental governance and land management. Through this work we have seen an increasing recognition of the impacts of increased privatisation of public spaces and the critical role of land ownership and management. Alongside this, a wave of movements, projects and initiatives is emerging that identify key principles that challenge the monopoly of control and the constant push to profits over community life.

In some respects this is perhaps a new paradigm – one based on the common good, on a regenerative economy supporting sustainable livelihoods, and on a new, replenishing relationship between people and the environment. These movements are coming from a number of areas. From the public sector, these include the 'new municipalists' and the community wealth-building approach at the heart of the 'Preston Model', which has seen local authorities using their assets to boost local revenue and keep money flowing locally.

Increasing concerns about the unaccountable nature of the management of the shared and community spaces in new housing developments is also driving a growing focus on the development of long-term stewardship models that are not only financially sustainable in the long term but are genuinely accountable to local people and owned and controlled by community-led organisations.

The CLT movement is growing rapidly as more communities are taking the provision of local affordable housing into their own hands. There are now over 290 CLTs in England, half of which were created in the past two years, acting as long-term stewards of housing, ensuring that it remains genuinely affordable, based on what people actually earn in their area, not just for now but in the future, effectively decommodifying land and housing in their control.

Food growing is another area where communities are increasingly taking control of land in order to meet demand for fresh, locally grown produce and to provide employment and training. Abandoned allotments, disused local authority plant nurseries, underused spaces in parks and estates are being cultivated to meet basic needs and provide spaces for people to connect and learn together. There is a thriving food-growing sector in London and other cities like Bristol, Manchester and Sheffield, and significant opportunities provided by peri-urban land to grow food at scale. Our recent research into the current state of local authority–owned farmland also shows that some (albeit a minority) of English councils are actively building on the connections between locally grown food and local social, economic and environmental resilience.

Several current projects also extend beyond the urban – or even the peri-urban – to challenge our conceptions of the relationship between town and countryside and to shift our ideas about community control from the neighbourhood to the landscape scale. In the Welsh Valleys we have worked with partners led by The Green Valleys to explore the potential for these areas to take control of the landscape that surrounds their towns to provide sustainable livelihoods, renewable resources and a new identity for local people as long-term stewards of the landscape beyond their homes and streets.

In Scotland, where a proactive legislative programme of land reform has been firmly framed in terms of community empowerment and locally led social and economic regeneration, over half a million acres of land are in community ownership. While this has largely been a rural movement to date, the Scottish

Land Commission is actively looking at how land reform can be enacted in an urban context, focusing in particular on the impacts on communities of vacant and derelict land and how it can be brought back into use in ways that serve the interests and needs of local people. New models of organising both individuals and organisations are also proliferating, supporting people to proactively take control of different parts of their lives. The community organising methodologies used by the Company of Community Organisers and Citizens UK offer powerful ways of getting to the heart of local issues. NEON supports people organising for a new and more just economy to work more effectively and network better together. We are partners in CtrlShift – a movement of organisations coming together to rethink how we take back control. Similarly the Land Justice Network and others are increasingly drawing the attention of activists and communities to the pernicious effects of our current land system – and starting interesting conversations about what rights we all need over the land around us, and what responsibilities landowners should have.

Action for a Fairer Urban Land Future

All three of the ideas below start with the assumption that land should be seen as a commonly-held resource for all wherever it is possible to do so. These ideas enable people to act on a space, rather than make them passive consumers of it.

National and Regional Land-Use Strategies

Historically, cities drew on their hinterlands for food and resources. Globalisation has increasingly broken that link, but the need to transition rapidly to a zero-carbon economy and increasing food insecurity as a result of Brexit opens up opportunities to expand existing peri-urban food initiatives and create new ones. The need for large-scale reforestation also means we are likely to see large swathes of new woodland created around towns and cities with opportunities for new livelihoods, recreation and the production of timber and other woodland products. The Green Belts that surround many of our larger cities are already protected against development but current policy is silent on how the land we are protecting in this way is managed, with much of it being given up to unproductive uses such as horse grazing or golf courses. Without a land-use strategy or framework in place, developed by democratically accountable government at the national and local level, we are unable to encourage and incentivise uses and forms of management that put local people in control and meet local needs.

A Right to Public Space

England has a relatively limited rural 'Right to Roam', but our ability to act as free citizens in our urban spaces is increasingly constrained. 'POPS' or Privately Owned Public Spaces are constrained in terms of rights of assembly, protest and use, even often including the right to take photos. Often this is not well understood or publicised, and recent revelations about the use of facial recognition at Granary Square in London show that even local authorities do not often know the full extent of the control mechanisms private operators install. The Campaign to Protect Rural England (CPRE) and others are starting interesting work on this (and a *Public London Charter*, in which the city's public spaces would operate with the minimum of rules to ensure open and accessible space for all, is being drafted by the Greater London Assembly). We would echo the call for a shared set of rights of access to, and use of, public open space that apply whoever owns it.

A Community Right to Buy

The 2011 Localism Act in England introduced a Community Right to Bid, allowing communities and parish councils to nominate buildings or land for listing by the local authority as an asset of community value. If the assets comes up for sale, the community can 'pause' the sale and take up to six months to find the funding required to buy the asset. However, in Scotland a much stronger Community Right to Buy gives communities first refusal when a piece of land is put on the market, and to buy land that is abandoned, neglected or causing harm to the environmental well-being of the community, even where the owner does not wish to sell. This provides a powerful reinforcement of the principle that underpins the Scottish land reform movement, that landowners not only have rights over how they use their land, but responsibilities to the wider community for the impacts and consequences of their management or mismanagement of it.

Notes

1. L. Lees, P. Hubbard and N. Tate, *Gentrification, Displacement, and the Impacts of Council Estate Renewal in C21st London.* Economic and Social Research Council, 2017–2020. Accessed 18 April 2020. https://gtr.ukri.org/projects?ref=ES%2FN015053%2F1.
2. P. Hubbard and L. Lees, 'The Right to Community: Legal Geographies of Resistance on London's Final Gentrification Frontier', *CITY* 22(1) (2018): 8–25.
3. H. Sheffield, 'Are Community Land Trusts a Way Out of the System?' *Red Pepper*, 17 October 2019. Accessed 18 April 2020. https://www.redpepper.org.uk/are-community-land-trusts-a-way-out-of-the-system/.

4   J. Steele, 'Self Renovating Neighbourhoods as an Alternative to Gentrification or Decline', in *Handbook of Gentrification Studies*, ed. L. Lees with M. Phillips, 467–80 (Cheltenham: Edward Elgar, 2018).
5   A. Amin, D. Massey and N. Thrift, *Cities for the Many, Not the Few* (Bristol: Policy Press, 2000).
6   'The Value of Land and Housing in London'. Greater London Authority, 2016. Accessed 18 April 2020. https://www.london.gov.uk/sites/default/files/chapter4-economic-evidence-base-2016.pdf#targetText=Residential%20land%20values%20in%20London,Brent%20to%2015%20in%20Westminster.
7   B. Christophers, *The New Enclosure: The Appropriation of Public Land in Neoliberal Britain* (London: Verso, 2018).
8   'Rising Burden of Housing Costs Shown by 60-Year UK Spending Survey'. *Financial Times*, 18 January 2018. Accessed 18 April 2020. https://www.ft.com/content/32d71316-fc5f-11e7-9b32-d7d59aace167.

Chapter 9

THE UNRAVELLING CITY

FACING THE PUBLIC SERVICES CRISIS

Annette Hastings

Before the Crisis

Once there was a time when there was little interest in public services, either from academic researchers or from the wider public. In the post-war period in the United Kingdom, we came to take it for granted that libraries would be open and well stocked, refuse collected, streets cleaned, the elderly cared for. It seemed that for most people, most of the time, decent public services were part and parcel of daily life, there in the background, sometimes provoking a grumble from time to time, but not in crisis.

Then along came the New Labour Government. In the first decade of the 2000s, we learned that public services were not working well for everyone: in particular, that they were failing people living in disadvantaged parts of cities. We already knew of course that post-war urban development had marooned some people in ill-conceived, poorly maintained social housing estates. But in this period, we learned that not everyone enjoyed the range and standard of public services that underpin quality of life and make neighbourhoods work well for people. The Social Exclusion Unit proclaimed that public services were key weapons in the battle against urban deprivation. In a period characterised by growing investment in public services across the board, specific targets, initiatives and investments were developed with the aim of trying to ensure that local services worked better for those living in disadvantaged circumstances.

While the evidence on the success of this activity is mixed, it is perhaps important to recall the ambition and energy, the sense of potential and hope that existed in relation to public services not so very long ago. In briefly sketching some aspects of 'before the crisis', I aim to evoke that sense of hope. I also aim to remind us that, even when public services are not in crisis, they do not always work best for those who need them most. A third aim is to put front and centre the ideas that when services unravel, it is the poor and vulnerable who suffer the most. Better off groups can substitute the bookshop for the library, the private gym for the municipal leisure centre. Elites can withdraw to gated communities with built-in security and maintenance services, as well as to private schools and private healthcare. People living with poverty and disadvantage rely pretty much entirely on the infrastructure of public service provision. The agenda for change in this chapter tries to take account of these issues.

The Crisis

But first the crisis. In relation to public services, the second decade of the 2000s could hardly have been more different from the first. While austerity cuts have affected almost all public services – schools, police, healthcare – it is the extent of the cuts to council budgets that has ensured that the public service crisis is, in large part, an urban crisis. As the Centre for Cities (2019) reported, it is cities that have borne the largest proportion of council budget cuts. Thus, people living in English cities are experiencing an annual spending cut of £386 per head to their council services, compared to £172 per head in areas outwith cities, despite greater levels of need.[1] And, as is well known, northern cities have seen the highest relative cuts while some in the south have escaped almost unscathed (although it is worth noting that London has experienced by far the biggest absolute cut). Cities in Scotland and Wales have generally fared less severely than their English counterparts, although change in spending in Glasgow is similar to, or indeed greater than, that affecting many English Northern cities.

So what do these statistics mean for people and places within cities? The National Audit Office (2018)[2] gives us an overview of some important changes in services and outcomes in England between 2010 and 2016. Council-run bus services had almost halved their mileage since 2010, one in ten libraries had closed, a third more households were defined as officially homeless and fly-tipping was up by more than 20 per cent. While the funding crisis in English schools has attracted lots of attention – with stories in the press of teachers cleaning schools to balance budgets – non-school education budgets which support early years (e.g. Sure Start) and youth services provision have been cut by more than half and 65 per cent, respectively (p. 27 of the National Audit Office report). But it is the social care crisis, particularly as it affects the growing elderly population, that has grabbed most of the headlines and – indeed – has secured a degree of budgetary protection, albeit that resources remain out of step with burgeoning needs. However, as with schools, the focus on elderly care has perhaps been at the expense of attention to the crisis in other spheres of social care and social work. For example, the National Audit Office reported that the Supporting People budget, which provides housing-related support to the most vulnerable, is the service area which has been most drastically cut during austerity – by 70 per cent by 2016.

And how do people experience using such pared down services? Research I and colleagues undertook for the Joseph Rowntree Foundation in four urban areas in England and Scotland gives an insight into what it's like to be at the front line of austerity, especially for those who are already materially disadvantaged.[3] In two of these cities, young parents told of social isolation as the result of changes in the cost of bus services after they were re-contracted to save money. One suggested that 'going anywhere that is not walking distance is a treat for me', while another young mum told us that she had 'stopped taking the baby out'. We were told that libraries had not only closed, but that opening hours of those that remained open had also been cut. As important to those working in and using the services of libraries was the strong sense that their role in the community was changing: rather than being there primarily to provide books and information, they had become places at the front line of welfare reform, supporting the job search requirements of the Department for Work and Pensions (DWP) and providing shelter for homeless people and others with complex needs, as other support (often funded via the Supporting People budget) was withdrawn.

It was also made clear that the condition of local neighbourhoods was also deteriorating – particularly in parks, playgrounds and open spaces. Here the effects not just of the increased fly-tipping noted by the National Audit Office, but of reduced grass cutting and litter picking regimes were evident. It seemed that this kind of deterioration can have quite a large impact on neighbourhoods and those who live in them. It had led to the loss of other services, for example. A play leader explained that they had had to withdraw their service from one area: 'We couldn't use the space [...] it wasn't clean, it wasn't fit for the children to use [...] the dog poo, the broken glass or possibly worse, syringes or whatever.' Parents also told of how they or their children had stopped using some playgrounds and parks. In three of the cities, residents highlighted increased problems with vermin, and in two, reduced street lighting had led to changes in walking routes and fewer trips out after dark. Once again it seemed to be children and young people who suffered the most as a result – we met parents who suggested that they no longer allowed their children to walk to evening activities and so could no longer attend.

A number of the focus groups held as part of this research took place in children's centres and involved young parents who clearly valued these early-years services. Many of those living in particularly disadvantaged or challenging circumstances described their role in their lives as transformational, providing access to expert advice, social support and respite. But it seemed that austerity had rendered these services precarious. Some centres had closed and services and clients moved to other centres, some of which were difficult to access. We were also told that professional staff – health visitors, psychologists, speech therapists – were no longer available at centres or that routine play sessions were cancelled or had become overcrowded as the result of staff shortages. Some of these young parents also relayed their concerns about social care for elderly relatives, as did some of the older people who took part in the research. The extent to which care provided to older people at home was critical for their well-being was very clear, but its fragility was also in evidence. Concerns were experienced about staff turnover and continuity as well as problems with different services connecting with one another. Discussions with care workers and other front line workers revealed the precarity of services most acutely, however. They described how at times they simply lacked the capacity to meet needs, particularly of the most vulnerable, or were unable to connect together different services for those with complex needs. As one housing officer told us, 'People know about vulnerable individuals […] they're left, they ignore them, and then you find them six months later or a year later.'

Getting Out of the Crisis

So how do we get out of this crisis? Moving away from this sense of crisis is not simply a matter of more resources – although it is essential that there is sustained, substantial reinvestment in the range of public services that underpin the well-being of most of us. My three suggestions for action are not therefore focused on refinancing public services, but rather on rebuilding a sense of purpose for local services. They are designed to suggest ways in which public services can be a vehicle to build social solidarity and for tackling entrenched inequalities. Below I suggest three action points for policymakers:

1. Start talking about council services
2. Encourage and support Fairness Commissions
3. Embed tackling inequality into the work of local agencies

Start Talking about Council Services

A national conversation about the kind of public services we want and expect in our cities is long overdue. Some issues get lots of air time and are part of public discourse. In relation to public services, the National Health Service (NHS) and adult social care fit into this category. In 2018, the UK Parliament established its first Citizens' Assembly to consider the long-term funding of adult social care. Fifty people, largely representative of the population as a whole, heard expert testimony over two weekends and then developed a set of recommendations which fed into a parliamentary inquiry, offering a view on what kind of care system people might be prepared to pay for.

Perhaps we need local Citizens' Assemblies in towns and cities across the country, established to debate similar issues with regard to council services more generally? Do we still want and need a collectively funded infrastructure of local services? If so, which services are important, who would get them, who would pay, how much? And so on. There is plenty to discuss and debate. These local assemblies would need to be designed not only to stimulate conversations within urban areas, but also to feed into a national process which could inform the Westminster and devolved governments in relation to decisions about resourcing and supporting such services.

If we don't start talking about local public services, considering their value and debating their worth, they might just gradually wither away without us realising that they are going, and without an opportunity to reflect on what would happen if they were gone.

Encourage and Support Fairness Commissions

A number of Fairness Commissions have been established in the past few years, with the aim of developing policy recommendations designed to tackle poverty and inequality. While Commissions have made numerous and diverse recommendations focused on what the private and voluntary sectors can do, almost all Commissions have recognised the central, transformative role which local public services play in urban areas.

A wide range of action has been recommended by Commissions: from the mainstreaming of inclusive growth principles in all public investments in North Lanarkshire, to improving transport affordability in Sheffield, to tackling the stigma of poverty in Dundee. Fairness Commissions often set out to build a sense of solidarity between different social groups, partly achieved by making it clear that everyone has something to gain from investing in and improving local public services – but at the same time recognising that fairness means that the most benefit must be gained by those most in need of support. Local Citizens' Assemblies could of course feed into Fairness Commissions, or could be established to take forward their recommendations in ways that support consensus and solidarity.

Embed Tackling Inequality into the Work of Local Agencies

The so-called Socio-economic Duty provided for in the 2010 Equality Act requires public services to ensure that their strategic decisions take account of the need to reduce inequalities in outcome that derive from socio-economic disadvantage. The duty has not been activated in England, despite being called for by the Equality and Human Rights Commission and the UN Committee on Economic, Social and Cultural Rights. However – offering hope – the Duty was brought into force in Scotland as the Fairer Scotland Duty in April 2018, a development which has been endorsed in the National Assembly for Wales. In the meantime, Newcastle City Council has decided to act as if the duty does already apply.[4] Among other things, this means assessing its own budgetary decisions for their impact on people vulnerable to socio-economic disadvantage, such as people living in deprived areas, or looked-after children.

Activating the socio-economic duty clearly signals an intention to ensure that public services work best for the poorest and more vulnerable in society. It is a way of ensuring that post-crisis public services will not have some of the problems of pre-crisis services – this time round, they will work best for those who need them the most. More than that, though, where public agencies do succeed in tackling aspects of inequality, they will also reduce the level of need for services, with long term gains for all.

RESISTING THE NEW NORMAL

Julian Dobson

In the summer of 2017, I met Debbie Stephens, chief executive of the L30 Community Centre in Netherton, a low-rise post-war estate on the northern fringe of Liverpool. I was there to discover how local people were starting to rebuild community with the help of a £1m Big Local grant. What she told me highlighted how hard it is to build community when the infrastructure that supports it is coming apart.

She recalled a shooting that had taken place right outside the community centre. The victim was still lying on the ground when volunteers began arriving for a meeting of the Big Local steering group. She described a night when around twenty young people were 'running wild' on the roof of the community centre and she was alone inside. Worried that they would get violent, she called the police – only to be told nobody was available to help. Garry McCartney, local area coordinator for Sefton Council, explained to me: 'They don't do preventive policing now and the youths in the area know that. The youths know there's no police helicopter anymore. There was a fire in the park and the youths just bricked the fire brigade.'[5]

Absent policing can be the most visible and visceral sign of the dismantling of public services through nearly a decade of austerity. There are other visible signs. The number of rough sleepers on urban streets rose by 165 per cent in the eight years since 2010.[6] Towns and cities that used to provide effective crisis help are now overwhelmed and informal tent cities of homeless people are becoming part of urban life as they were in the 1990s. Library closures have been a striking example of public service decline, possibly because libraries are fortunate enough to have a small army of articulate middle-class defenders. Nonetheless, 449 libraries across the United Kingdom closed between 2012 and 2017. In 2018 the community network, Locality, reported that more than four thousand publicly owned assets have been moved into private ownership every year since 2012.[7] In 2017 MPs reported that council-owned parks and green spaces were at a 'tipping point' of decline.[8] More than five-hundred council-run children's centres in England closed between 2010 and 2018. The clear loss to many communities is palpable and problematic.

Sometimes the signs of attrition are less visible. Libraries may still be open, but that may be because they are now run by unpaid volunteers or local charities. It is estimated that at least 580 such libraries now exist across the United Kingdom. Community centres may still be there, but the activities they hosted for teenagers or elderly people may have stopped. The police and fire services may still arrive in an emergency, but aren't around to provide the presence and advice that reassures a community that all is, if not well, at least under some semblance of control.

The invisible deterioration of public services attracts little attention, but away from public scrutiny a quiet unravelling is taking place. If environmental health inspectors don't enforce food hygiene regulations as they used to, does anybody notice the fall in prosecutions? A report by Unison, the public services union, found the number of environmental health inspections fell by 40 per cent over the last decade.[9] The Chartered Institute of Environmental Health reported a 25 per cent fall over the same period in housing safety inspections. If a local authority lacks the capacity to enforce planning regulations, does anyone outside the conservation lobby pay attention? If the local leisure centre cuts its opening hours, how are these effects experienced? We are compelled to ask: How long does it take before we accept a new normal of services that are withering or have disappeared?

Forged by Neglect: The New Normal

Back in 2010, the coalition government attempted to create a new approach to the losses incurred through austerity by making its rhetoric about localism and the 'Big Society' its acceptable face: yes, there would be 'necessary' cuts to rebalance public finances, but it was an opportunity for communities to step into the gap and take control of local assets and services. It didn't take long for the Big Society ideal to melt in the face of swingeing cuts to the very community organisations that were expected to hold the fort for a new generation of agile, enabling – and, most importantly, slimmed-down – public service commissioners.

Cuts to capacity, however, took time to work their way through to frontline services and the fabric of buildings and places. The lagging effect of public service cuts allowed government to compound the reductions year after year: between 2010 and 2017/2018, central government funding for English local authorities fell by 49.1 per cent in real terms, and spending power (taking locally raised resources into account) fell by 28.6 per cent. At the same time demand was rising, forcing councils to focus on an increasingly narrow range of statutory services, with social care consuming the lion's share of budgets.[10] Only occasionally did the cumulative reductions in public services grab public attention. A particularly revealing episode came in 2015 when the then prime minister, David Cameron, wrote to Oxfordshire Council to protest at cuts in day centres, libraries and museums in his constituency, apparently oblivious that his own chancellor had cut grants to the authority by 37 per cent.

Senior politicians' ignorance of the effects of their own decisions is telling. Those who do not depend day-to-day on public services only notice this essential infrastructure when it stops working. The new normal they have created is likely to persist, despite recent proclamations of the end of austerity, because even if cuts are reversed it takes years to rebuild. The most recent promise of 20,000 new police officers won't affect crime levels until they have been recruited, trained and learned to know their patch; and in the meantime nobody is promising to fund the unsung workhorses of public service, the planners and environmental health officers and children's workers.

Four aspects of the new normal should give particular cause for concern.

First is the notion that any degree of decline can be offset through innovation rather than core funding and continuing financial support. This is not to say that innovation is in itself problematic; nor is it to denigrate the creative thinking that has arisen from the crucible of austerity. But innovation can become a way of avoiding confrontation rather than addressing challenges. Take parks and green spaces, which are particularly vulnerable to cuts and neglect because there is no statutory duty to provide and look after them. Recent years have seen an increasing focus on 'rethinking parks' – broadly speaking, trying to find roundabout ways of continuing to provide public benefits without creating public responsibilities. Charitable foundations are funding efforts to identify alternative forms of funding and management – from setting up charitable trusts to an increasing emphasis on commercial activities that risk turning parks into playgrounds for the affluent. We need reminding that newness isn't always progress, and must be judged by benchmarks of equality and accountability as well as inventiveness.

Second is the erosion of capacity. Efficiency is too often seen in terms of reduced headcounts and not in terms of effective services. In Nottingham I interviewed a woman whose role was to advise schools on energy efficiency, helping them to work more effectively and save money. But the funding for her job was about to end, and she admitted her main concern now was how she would pay her mortgage. Erasing roles like these may not cause immediate harm, but it removes opportunities for improvement. What's lost is never seen because it was never permitted to arrive.

Third, and connected to the erosion of capacity, is the cumulative loss of institutional learning. Sometimes you can watch this as it happens. Shortly after the coalition took office, a particularly controversial programme known as Housing Market Renewal was abruptly scrapped. For all its failings, the programme also generated important understandings of how (and how not) to intervene in neighbourhoods characterised by 'low demand' for homes. A housing worker in Oldham told me how his team was disbanded and he was re-employed by the local council. He asked what should be done with the numerous local studies his project had commissioned. 'Put them in the skip' was the response. Learning is lost, too, when there are fewer resources for people to continue their professional training, when staff take redundancy or early retirement in cost-cutting exercises and when institutional memory is fragmented by constant reorganisation, changes of leadership or closure.

Connected to all three of these issues is a tendency to repeat the mistakes of the past. In early 2019 I took part in a project to identify key lessons from evaluations of regeneration programmes over the past two decades. Some themes recurred with an insistent drumbeat: build local capacity before spending money, get governance and accountability right, continue for long enough to make a difference and give careful thought to what you leave when you've gone. The so-called end of austerity and loosening of financial purse-strings risks repeating every mistake from the regeneration programmes of the 1990s. Local funds are offered on dubious criteria to show something is being done about a problem; money is offered in the form of capital pots to be spent on buildings and engineering rather than people; and cash goes to expensive consultants rather than into local economies because the networks of local public services have been stripped to the bone. A few years ago a development worker in Huddersfield showed me a litter bin with a logo from a regeneration programme that had ended a decade previously. The bin was the only visible sign that the neighbourhood had been regarded as a government priority. Unless we challenge new spending, as well as cuts in spending, we risk investing in the logo-encrusted bins of the future.

Putting Public Service Back on the Agenda

Amid the neglect and damage, there are hopeful signs. They need to be kept in perspective – if a new world is being made in the shell of the old, it is a long time coming – but I would highlight four areas where there is a growing appetite for change.

First is the serious consideration of how green spaces can be part of a natural health service, supporting the well-being of urban populations and at the same time addressing the challenges of a climate and biodiversity crisis. Amid some of the clutching at straws taking place among council parks departments, some are taking time to creatively rethink the idea of a park as a place where stressed individuals and households can find respite, friendship and a connection with nature (recognising that humans are an integral part of nature). Camden and Islington councils are examining how their green spaces can meet public health objectives; in Rotherham eight miles of roadside verges have been planted to create a 'river of flowers' to support biodiversity and turn drab central reservations and roundabouts into places of joy and colour.

Second is the work being done through organisations like the Big Local schemes to rebuild local services from the ground up, creating spaces and activities that meet the changing needs of communities rather than working to tired templates of how things should be done. Such work recognises the value of putting conversation first rather than investing in shiny new facilities that don't stay shiny for long. Other initiatives using a 'conversation-first' approach and building on the strengths and interests of local people include the Participatory City project in Barking, east London, working with 25,000 local residents to generate neighbourhood-led projects. But such approaches must be additional to, not a substitute for, core public services as has been the case over the past decade and more.

More strategically significant is the work done in Preston to use the still substantial clout of public service 'anchor' organisations to support the local economy, trading with local suppliers and using public service purchasing power to strengthen community infrastructure, and paying public sector workers (including those working for contractors) a living wage. This is just one example of a suite of initiatives that go under the umbrella term of community wealth-building, and put public services back at the heart of local prosperity. Work to develop alternatives to the siphoning of community cash through platforms like Uber or Amazon is also important, with increasing interest in co-operative versions anchored in the community.

Connecting locality with society, the growing interest in Universal Basic Income shows how a top-down, welfarist approach to public service could be reimagined to empower individuals and households to work in ways that provide real value and choice for themselves and their communities. Some have argued that rather than experimenting with a basic income, we should have universal basic services – a set of standard services such as education and healthcare to which every citizen is unconditionally entitled. We need both types of reform, recognising that the first – a level of income that provides the necessities of life and enables people to exercise choice about how they work – may reduce pressures on the second. At the same time we need to recognise that 'universal' services must be human rather than bureaucratic. Universality should not imply uniformity. Responsive, person-centred and flexible services that allow people to find appropriate solutions to the challenges of precarity are required for twenty-first-century urban life.

Thinking about these signs of hope in the light of the lessons from the past suggests an agenda for action. Of the many possible actions policymakers could take, perhaps three could be particularly effective:

1. Put people before stuff. In other words, match capital funding with revenue funding to invest in the people who bring places to life. Investment in buildings or spaces is only as good as the investment in the people who animate and look after them. This is a message for all public sector funders, as well as charitable and philanthropic foundations.
2. Enrich social infrastructure. Public sector and government organisations, from local government to the NHS, should invest in the community-based

networks and organisations that provide social support and take the pressure off frontline services. Done properly, this supports effective local services.
3. Couple universal basic services with universal basic income. This is a long-term ask of national government, but trials could begin now. The goal should be to find participatory, democratic ways to give citizens more say in the services they receive. Deliberative processes such as participatory budgeting and citizens' assemblies should be used to steer and shape the thinking of decision-makers and elected politicians, at local level and nationally.

Notes

1 Centre for Cities. *Cities Outlook 2019*. Centre for Cities, 2019. Accessed 19 April 2020. https://www.centreforcities.org/wp-content/uploads/2019/01/19-01-28-Cities-Outlook-2019-Full.pdf.
2 National Audit Office. *Financial Sustainability of Local Authorities 2018*. NAO, 2018. Accessed 19 April 2020. https://www.nao.org.uk/report/financial-sustainability-of-local-authorities-2018/.
3 A. Hastings et al., 'The Cost of the Cuts: The Impact on Local Government and Poorer Communities'. Joseph Rowntree Foundation, 2015. Accessed 19 April 2020. https://www.jrf.org.uk/report/cost-cuts-impact-local-government-and-poorer-communities.
4 Just Fair. *Tackling Socio-Economic Inequalities Locally*. Just Fair, June 2018. Accessed 19 April 2020. http://justfair.org.uk/wp-content/uploads/2018/06/Just-Fair-June2018-Tackling-socio-economic-inequalities-locally.pdf.
5 J. Dobson, *New Seeds beneath the Snow? Big Local Neighbourhoods in Action*. Local Trust, 2018. Accessed 19 April 2020. https://localtrust.org.uk/insights/essays/new-seeds-beneath-the-snow-an-essay-by-julian-dobson/.
6 'Rough Sleepers: Access to Services and Support'. House of Commons Library, 9 October 2019. Accessed 19 April 2020. https://researchbriefings.parliament.uk/ResearchBriefing/Summary/CBP-7698.
7 Locality. *The great British sell off*. Locality, 2018). Accessed 19 April 2020. https://locality.org.uk/wp-content/uploads/2018/06/The-Great-British-Sell-Off-FINAL.pdf.
8 House of Commons Communities and Local Government Committee. *Public Parks: Seventh Report of Session 2016–17*. House of Commons, 30 January 2017. Accessed 19 April 2020. https://publications.parliament.uk/pa/cm201617/cmselect/cmcomloc/45/45.pdf.
9 'Environmental Health: How Cuts Are Putting Individuals and Communities at Risk and Damaging Local Businesses and Economies'. Unison. Accessed 10 October 2019. https://www.unison.org.uk/content/uploads/2019/04/Damage-environmental-health.pdf.
10 National Audit Office. *Financial Sustainability of Local Authorities 2018*. NAO, 2018. Accessed 19 April 2020. https://www.nao.org.uk/report/financial-sustainability-of-local-authorities-2018/.

Chapter 10

THE UNACCOUNTABLE CITY

AN UNFINISHED DEMOCRACY

Simin Davoudi

Introduction

To understand cities, we need to know their politics. It is not a coincidence that the term politics comes from the Greek word *polis*. The significance of polis in the evolution of urban politics lies in its citizens' practice of direct democracy. Today's representative democracies are arguably the legacies of that ancient practice. Although it is often translated into city-state, *polis* has a broader meaning which, according to Aristotle, refers to a milieu within which citizens can realise their moral and intellectual capacities, their life chances and their sense of social belonging. In short, the polis was the embodiment of hope. But, as in contemporary cities, it was also the epitome of despair, not least for women and slaves who were not considered to be citizens and did not have the right to vote for decisions on urban affairs. I aim to engage with these paradoxical possibilities in this chapter by focusing on democracy and localism.

Democracy: An Unfinished Business

> The last 30 years have seen a number of important institutions fall from grace very publicly. [...] The banking sector, the press and politicians are all now judged far more critically than they were in the early 1980s, and there is a clear sense that people have lost faith in some of Britain's most important institutions. This certainly applies to politicians and the political process.[1]

Democracy can be a source of both hope and despair. While its promise of self-governing societies offers emancipatory hopes, its more limited representative version leads to despair. Today's political crisis is largely a manifestation of the widening gulf between the ideal of democracy and how it is actually practiced. People's everyday experience of democracy gives them the feeling that they are less and less in control of how their lives are governed, and by whom. Only 15 per cent of people across the United Kingdom believe that they have influence over national decisions.[2]

This has generated widespread frustrations with conventional politics, elite politicians and established political parties, as the above quote from the British Social Attitudes (BSA) survey shows. Whatever limited trust people had in public institutions is being further eroded, and public confidence in their ability to strive for common good, fairer society and better life opportunities is diminishing. While in 1986, 38 per cent trusted 'governments to put the nation's needs above those of a political party', by 2011, BSA found that 'only one in five' (18 per cent) did so.

Disaffections with political elites raise questions over democratic legitimacy and accountability of established political institutions. There is a growing disjuncture between the stage-managed political theatres that the elites engage in, and are projected on television screens and social media, and the reality of people's everyday political struggles to be heard and represented. Rising political apathy and falling participation in local and national elections are among the most troubling signs of contemporary political crises, because they are indicative of a democracy that is losing its *demos* and being hollowed out. To quote BSA again, in 1987 '76 per cent believed that "it's everyone's duty to vote"'. That figure fell to 62 per cent by 2011 and is likely to be lower today.

At a broader, philosophical level, we can find the root causes of discontents in the inherent tensions in Western democracies between the ideal of self-governed free individuals and the practical need for political authorities that govern social relations and maintain social order. What we are witnessing today is widespread feelings that the balance between these two opposing forces has swung too far, away from governing ourselves towards being governed; from being in charge of our lives towards losing control and submitting our futures to the invisible hands of the market and/or unaccountable governments. The social contract is losing its appeal.

Several recent events have exacerbated these feelings. Core among them are years of economic austerity; cutbacks in public services; welfare reforms; global population displacement and migration crises; and the (Brexit) referendum on Britain's membership of the European Union, with its subsequent political wrangling. Together, these have led to a heightened sense of insecurity and precarity and the unsettling of people's sense of their identities, belongings and citizenships.

Precarious life and the lack of job security and prospects for better futures tear apart individuals' sense of social belonging. They create resentment, political indifference and erosion of trust in established democratic institutions. They fracture the democratic ties between represented and representative, and bring into question the legitimacy of representative democracy. Thus, the representatives (such as Eton-educated politicians) are no longer imagined to resemble the public they represent. Neither are they seen as speaking on their behalf (instead of regurgitating party political lines); standing for their interests (instead of their own political careers) nor delivering what the public need (notably a better quality of life). The vacuum created by the breakdown of democratic legitimacies is being increasingly filled with populist movements and far-right parties that hijack peoples' legitimate discontent with the status quo and turn it into an instrument of their regressive and divisive political agendas.

There is, however, a paradox. These growing frustrations with democracy have been happening at the time when British politics has been endowed with a decade of localism and its promise of democratisation. Why is that so?

Localism: Promised Land or the Offloading of Responsibilities?

Localism is an elusive concept whose remarkable discursive power lies in its ability to speak to a whole spectrum of communitarian, liberal and libertarian political intents, and to offer remedies for a wide range of malaise. It promises local jobs and businesses in the face of globalising economies; small-scale and close-knit communities in the face of alienating societies; well-defined neighbourhoods in the face of shapeless, expanding cities; place-based identities in the face of place-less homogenising cultures; sustainability and self-sufficiency in the face of degrading ecologies and civic empowerment in the face of centralising polity. However, despite their 'warm glow', these remedies are infused with tensions and contradictions and can engender regressive and perverse outcomes, as the 10 years of localism in Britain has shown.[3]

On taking office in 2010, the Conservative–Liberal Democrat coalition government made so-called localism and 'Big Society' the central plank of its political agenda, based on rationales similar to those mentioned above. These are clearly reflected in the then government's statement:

> There's the *efficiency* argument that in huge hierarchies, money gets spent on bureaucracy instead of the frontline. There is the *fairness* argument that centralised national blueprints don't allow for local solutions to major social problems. And there is the political argument that centralisation creates a distance in our *democracy* between the government and the governed (emphasis added).[4]

Localism was propelled into the political limelight as the solution for the problems of an inefficient, unfair and undemocratic state. However, since then, there has been a growing concern not only with the unfulfilled promises, but more crucially with the legitimation of the regressive policies that have been introduced under the banner of localism.

In the name of *efficiency*, a decade of austerity has drastically reduced urban governments' human and financial resources and their capacity to meet the needs of their citizens. Contrary to the claims made in the above quotation, austerity measures have reduced the frontline services (such as social and adult care, local police, education and urban planning) that were supposed to be supported by tackling so-called bureaucracies.

In the name of *fairness*, 10 years of cuts in public expenditure have hit the most vulnerable social groups and the most deprived places in the country the hardest. Austerity measures have widened inequalities and exacerbated social and environmental injustices. In the name of finding local solutions for major social problems (such as poverty, homelessness, ill health and loneliness) government has off-loaded its responsibilities onto charitable, voluntary and faith-based organisations.

In the name of *democracy*, localism has bypassed democratically elected urban/local governments to create new hyper-local institutions such as neighbourhood planning forums which have largely benefitted the better-educated, better-off and more vocal groups. Worse, it has failed to empower grassroots communities or individual citizens to lead less precarious lives and more secure futures. Instead, the discourse of localism has been one of blaming, responsibilising and moralising. It suggests that to be a good citizen, individuals ought to be self-reliant, entrepreneurial, and responsible for their own destiny, irrespective of social and structural constraints that are outside their control. Communities, portrayed as the so-called true form of collectivity and bounded in small distinct areas, are moralised to become responsible for their own conducts and their own fates.

Finally, although localism has been invoked through the discourses of decentralisation, devolution and empowerment, in practice, central government has firmly held onto the steering wheel and in many areas of public affairs, such as local planning decisions, has even increased its powers to call the shots.

Spaces of Hope

None of the above should be read as if everything is doom and gloom. People might have lost trust and confidence in established political systems to deliver better quality of life, support them at times of hardship, or lead them in tackling social and ecological crises, but they have not lost faith in democracy or politics more generally. On the contrary, the BSA survey found political interest in 2013 was slightly higher than the mid-1980s and stood at 36 per cent, and people were more likely to have signed a petition or contacted their MPs.

Whether by design or by default, both austerity and localism have led to a growing sense of social solidarity and cooperation among citizens and communities. As earlier chapters have highlighted, up and down the country volunteers and charitable workers are compensating for the diminished safety nets that were previously provided by the public sector, and responding to the social and environmental crises that cities and citizens are facing. What is particularly promising is that many initiatives are not simply focused on crisis management and emergency responses (feeding the hungry, sheltering the homeless, etc.), important as these are. They are also engaged in building communities and networks, promoting solidarity, nurturing a sense of social belonging, and cultivating confidence and self-esteem.

Alongside these quiet activisms, there are also other forms of political movements at the local, national and global scales. In resisting unfair and undemocratic local planning decisions, unjust global extractions of resources and livelihoods, and authoritarian dictates, these movements are opening up spaces of hope for more democratic futures. They shine a beam of light on the paths towards fairer cities and societies.

An Agenda for Change

For democratic politics to function more effectively and at all levels, we need ambitious and transformative plans of action with multiple components of which the following three are most essential and urgent:

1. Mainstreaming participative democracies to complement representative democracies and become an integral part of decision-making processes. One way to do this is through the establishment of citizen assemblies in all cities and localities. These can work alongside the elected local politicians in making decisions about urban affairs.
2. Proactively developing civic capacities and supporting the public to make their voices not just heard, but also listened to, in the collective decisions that affect their lives. This requires, for example, ensuring access to information, facilitating social networking, encouraging political dialogues and promoting active citizenship.
3. Embarking on a consistent and comprehensive devolution of powers and resources to cities and localities in order to make elected representatives accountable to their local constituents and responsive to their local needs.

In conclusion, it is worth going back to the beginning and reiterating that democracy is an unfinished business in the sense that we can never be fully satisfied with democratic processes and outcomes. But this does not mean that democracy has to be all or nothing; either a fully participative process or a dictatorship cloaked in a democratic gown. Instead, democracy is itself a continuous process of invoking, energising and mobilising democratic principles in order to move towards the ideal of the government of the people, by the people and for the people.

DOES URBAN GOVERNMENT HAVE TO BE DESTRUCTIVE?

Jess Steele

Introduction

I approach this question from the bottom up and from the perspective of community power.

The fundamental characteristic of the urban is *density* which in turn both offers and requires collective action by people who are *proximate* – in other words they live, work and play in the space, thereby acting as the producers as well as consumers of the urban neighbourhood.

So the question for urban localism becomes: Are people able to make and protect places that serve their needs, reflect their interests and nurture their hopes? And if not, what is in the way?

I will argue that people are prevented from making good places because they don't have access to place-making resources and they can't participate in place-shaping decisions, and that these problems are exacerbated by the attitudes, rules and political cultures of urban government. Further, I suggest, perhaps controversially, that urban government has too often been a destructive and obstructive force undermining good urban place-making. It doesn't have to be like this, and the chapter ends with stories of hope and suggestions for how it might better be nurtured by urban governments.

Local Government and the Destruction of Places

Urban government has been implicated in the destruction of places, from post-war 'slum clearance' to the scorched earth regeneration of the Housing Market Renewal Programme which ended in 2011.

Sometimes the process is punitive and urban government teams up with the police or private security, housing associations and others, withdrawing services and increasing pressure on remaining residents. This process has its own fluctuating timescale – sometimes all of a rush, other times slow and painful like watching beams rot as water drips through the roof. Those timescales have nothing to do with the welfare of the people or the neighbourhood. Instead they are determined by two gaps – the 'rent gap' (the difference between current rents and the potential if put to 'highest and best use') and the 'agency gap' (the difference between people with a strong political voice and people with none).

Sometimes, as with Granby 4 Streets in Liverpool, the agency gap gets closed through the very process of resistance – community strength forged in the struggle. But more often people are 'decanted' and moved, places are wiped out. Sometimes new buildings emerge. Built by developers or housing associations, they are rarely much to celebrate. Sometimes the spaces are left empty as the regeneration programmes come and go. If they are open sites then nature, children and dog walkers begin to lay claim to the spaces, though this can only be provisional. More often they are hoarded up, another piece of neighbourhood out of bounds and seemingly untouchable.

Since the 1980s, local authorities have also been a significant contributor to the production of dereliction. Quantitative research would be useful but in my 30-year experience I have personally come across hundreds of examples of councils abandoning historic buildings, from Lewisham's libraries languishing on the 'Disposals List' in the early 1990s to the magnificent 1937 Flag Lane Baths in Crewe, closed over a weekend in April 2016 when the new Lifestyle Centre opened, and now rapidly deteriorating.

Buildings do not like being unoccupied and the costs of renovation rise exponentially over time. Unfortunately, with slashed resources, slow processes and many competing demands, time empty and unattended is exactly what councils gift these cast-offs. Meanwhile various delinquent private owners (gangsters, absentees, pension funds, the Crown) get away with leaving their buildings to rot because the legislation to prevent it and the political resources to mount a rescue depend entirely on local government intervention. For many years councils took 'the DER response' – *too difficult, too expensive, too risky*. Now they say 'would you rather we spent on children's services or notices to get the gutters fixed on a heritage building?' and there is no way to argue with that. The targeting of austerity at local government means that the system to prevent the mistreatment of the physical fabric of our towns and cities is all but defunct.

Municipal place-making was once a matter of great pride – witness the great town halls and civic infrastructure, even down to the flourishes on the humblest public conveniences. However, few urban governments have ever been very good at 'darning the fabric'. They have been too keen on the vanity mega-projects. The Victorians built beautiful buildings, but showed little remorse in demolishing ancient heritage. There have been some good examples of diligent conservation officers, confident lawyers or maverick councillors saving streets. But they are rare and seen as quirky. Our tax system, development planning, building control, professional egos and ultimately the financing of development, favour large-scale new build, so it is not surprising we tend to abandon or demolish rather than repurpose.

Urban governments are producing and maintaining physical dereliction. They are also deeply involved in regeneration as state-sponsored gentrification. Disinvestment sets up the rent gap and produces the opportunity.

Local authorities and developers write the copy between them ('X Project is *transforming* once-grim X Town'). Regeneration outputs no longer tend to include 'number of local authority dwellings demolished'[5] but they continue to focus on rises in house prices and rental yields. Eventually you learn to read underneath the words: as Loretta Lees has shown the benign-sounding 'mixed communities' policy was 'gentrification by stealth'.[6]

I would argue that such governmentality is anathema to neighbourhood, and that we know this intuitively to be the case, but we have put up with it for the sake of the greater democracy and central planning that we require at larger geographical scales.

Governmental timescales and relationships with place(s) are both problematic. Temporally, the inevitable focus on elections and development timescales overshadows both the human lifespan and the 'now and soon' which are critically important at neighbourhood level. Spatially, their place-frames – the way they view and understand places – are shaped by party political, technocratic and 'strategic' relationships that distort how they view neighbourhoods. In the absence of an adequate learning framework, they insist on endlessly reinventing the wheel. And in the wake of disfiguring cuts the urban government organisation shifts from former roles as funder or partner to become an active competitor for resources with communities themselves. The Wigan Deal is one approach that shows that it doesn't have to be like this. Fairer, cleverer and more successful than other local government responses to austerity, it remains an honourable exception.[7] In most places the 'gatekeepers' have been made redundant but the gates are firmly locked.

So why can't people at ground level – the producer-consumers of neighbourhood – get to shape their places actively and purposefully?

There are two major barriers: access to decision-making and access to resources.

Decisions That Make Place

The decision-making processes that shape neighbourhoods are opaque and accretive, building up layer upon layer, an odorous mixture of conspiracy, incompetence, inertia and track-covering.

A heavily contaminated ex-industrial site, empty and hoarded for 40 years, surrounded by homes in an area among the 1 per cent most deprived in England is owned by a dormant regeneration agency. The strategy has always been that the dereliction of the land will be 'solved' through private development and the poverty of the people will be 'solved' through social services. In 2016 a community organisation secures a licence on the land and works with local people to develop proposals that bring the land and the people back together through a community land trust – so that in rescuing the land, the people heal themselves and create tangible and sustainable community-owned assets for the future. A 'bottom-up development' (BUD) team of local people emerges from this work. They 'perform ownership' of the land through events and activities, maintenance and the development of shared resources (a tea hut, a stage, a pizza oven, a compost toilet). The positive shifts in individual well-being and collective agency are palpable. People who have felt powerless begin to see a way to make change together via the community land trust, owning land for the benefit of local people. However, the regeneration agency is both non-communicative and hostile. Although all three local authorities have seats on the board, they describe it as 'a private company' and allow its former chief executive to lead decision-making. An old-school 'regenerator' entirely focused on building a road to open up countryside land for development, he refuses to engage with the community land trust. The council is supportive but risk averse. They pay a consultant to explore options. He concludes the site is not viable without grant, but his report is never debated by councillors. Officers say they cannot take it to cabinet because they do not know what to recommend. After three years, the group are evicted to clear away 'any sign of community interest' so that the land can be 'market-tested' by one of the most expensive land agents in the country. The community land trust must bid for the land, even though it is clear that the only way a private sector interest could secure a profit would be to bank the site for another 10 years, wait for public investment in the rail infrastructure and then make a killing on the sale for commuter housing. There is no clarity about process or timescale and BUD team members are deeply frustrated but hardly surprised by the renewal of their customary powerlessness.

The dearth of resources for neighbourhoods that need them is founded on underlying problems of inequality, wastefulness and profit-skewed motivations. We are not a poor country but our resources – financial and human – need unlocking and harnessing for our common good. First, UK private household wealth (pensions and property) totals over £10 trillion. If those who are lucky enough to have unearned equity were able to use it for social good, just a tiny proportion would make a huge difference. Second, millions of our people are breaking their backs (physically or metaphorically) in hard, precarious work or chasing round a welfare system that keeps them busy, miserable and poor. We must face up to the coming transformation of 'work' and design a post-work future. Along with the effects of the climate emergency, this is surely an argument to give citizens more time and resource for the activity of 'making place locally'. Third, the dominant models for the ownership and development of land and buildings are actively antisocial. Henry George (1879[8]) argued that land value is created by society and should rightly be recaptured for society's use in the form of a land value tax. If citizens better understood the political economics of development as practiced in UK towns and cities today (a) they would be horrified and (b) they might be inspired to DIY approaches.

It is those DIY approaches that give me hope. All over the country, groups of local people are leading action of all kinds to 'darn the fabric' of their neighbourhoods – rescuing much-loved buildings, starting community businesses, developing shared resources and pioneering new types of placemaking. Two examples stand out because they combine lots of relatively small actions in fine-grain neighbourhoods with passionate articulations of how their work is driven by and contributes to a shared pro-social value base.

Granby 4 Streets

Emerging from decades of 'neighbourhood punishment' after the 1981 Toxteth Uprising (aka the Liverpool riots) and several years of stasis while the council sought a single developer for the whole neighbourhood, local residents formed a community land trust (CLT) that managed to shift the strategy towards a mixed approach in which the CLT played an *exemplary* role. They began by painting the tinned-up houses, filling the street with plants and benches, and developing a highly successful monthly market. They have now restored 11 houses, with a mix of social rent and covenant lease sales to protect permanent affordability. Two further houses were so far deteriorated they could not viably be used as residential accommodation and instead have been given a glass roof to create a 'Winter Garden' – a community space of superlative quality in this humble terraced street.

The Hastings Commons

Emerging organically from years of sustained community engagement, this holistic approach knits economic, social and cultural goals into the physical spaces of the neighbourhood. An 'ecosystem' of intertwined organisations linked by shared values see themselves as 'the tools in the box' to achieve their common goal: to create spaces for homes, work and leisure that will be affordable in perpetuity. They reject the 'false choice' of gentrification or dereliction, aiming to improve the neighbourhood *and* to protect its diversity through active inclusion and perpetually capped rents. Focused around an existing urban commons in the form of the Alley, a series of key buildings and spaces have been brought into 'custodian ownership' for the common good. Tenants are selected on the basis of need, local connection, enthusiasm for the ethos and willingness to contribute to the physical and social upkeep of the commons. Full ownership in the long term will rest with the Heart of Hastings community land trust.

These are examples of 'self-renovating neighbourhoods' – positive change initiated and driven by local people including explicit action to protect diversity through the freeholder power to set prices outside the market. They decommodify 'housing units' into homes and deconstruct landlord–tenant exploitation into a relationship of mutual support. Through caretaking in common they transform the meaning of ownership and belonging. David Harvey has argued that the right to the city is 'the right to change ourselves by changing the city'. The participants in self-renovating neighbourhoods become a new kind of *neighbourly*, not the cosy cup-of-sugar variety but a radical, sharp-edged version which recognises the need to build localised community power in order to reshape urban governance to be fit for purpose.

An Agenda for Change

If local urban government is to support positive change at neighbourhood level

1. Urban government should support local citizens to *build their own agency* so that they can actively make change in their lives and their neighbourhoods. This is not the 'Big Society' avoiding state responsibility; it is a matter of social justice, economic necessity and common good. It is the essence of initiatives like the Wigan Deal.
2. More innovative approaches to *unlocking private capital* for local social good should be tested, alongside and encouraged by government funding programmes that actively pursue best practice based on evidence and experience.
3. *Values-based collaborations* should be encouraged with the full participation of councillors and officers where invited. Which collaborations and to what end should be decided democratically and reported regularly to full council meeting in public.

Oh, and they should stop abandoning historic buildings just because they've managed to build a shiny new version!

Notes

1   BSA. *British Social Attitudes Survey 30, Key findings*. NatCen Social Research, 2013. Accessed 19 April 2020. http://www.bsa.natcen.ac.uk/media/1144/bsa30_key_findings_final.pdf.

2 Hansard Society. *Audit of Political Engagement 16: The 2019 Report.* Hansard Society, 2019. Accessed 19 April 2020. https://www.hansardsociety.org.uk/publications/reports/audit-of-political-engagement-16.
3 S. Davoudi and A. Madanipour, eds, *Reconsidering Localism* (London: Routledge, 2015).
4 HM Government. *The Localism Bill* (London: Stationary Office, 2010).
5 This was a genuine output measured on the K2 management system by Deptford City Challenge.
6 G. Bridge, T. Butler and L. Lees, *Mixed Communities: Gentrification by Stealth?* (Bristol: Policy Press, 2012).
7 The King's Fund. 'A Citizen-Led Approach to Health and Care: Lessons from the Wigan Deal'. The King's Fund, 26 June 2019. Accessed 19 April 2020. https://www.kingsfund.org.uk/publications/wigan-deal.
8 H. George, *Progress and Poverty: An Inquiry into the Cause of Increase of Want with Increase of Wealth, the Remedy* (New York: Cosimo, [1879] 2005).

Chapter 11

THE CHALLENGE OF CHANGE

Rowland Atkinson and Julian Dobson

Urban Crisis, Urban Hope is intended as a vocal challenge to the long-standing silence of UK urban policy. For too long, a lack of policy action or intervention has been compounded by massive declines in public investment and in support for the physical, social and environmental fabric of our towns and cities. As we write there is no explicit programme to ameliorate spatial inequalities, no assertion of the rights to a decent life and services for those in neighbourhoods without them, and little appetite in government to stitch together areas of knowledge and action across domains as diverse as welfare, housing, health, environment and criminal justice, all of which have overt and more subtle connections in the urban centres where they are played out. The contributors to this book note and celebrate the continual resurgence of grassroots activism, cooperative problem-solving and locally rooted struggles for change. But the deeper message of the volume demands a progressive, strategic, moderating and investing role for government. As a whole this book has highlighted the need for a much greater commitment to the resources required for policy to be devised and to be achievable.

We and our contributors join the voices of many others who consider the lived experience of inequality and declining environmental quality to be a standing injustice in a country that still ranks, despite the financial crisis of a decade ago, as among the richest in the world. But the poverty of these very measures of economic activity and pre-eminence is increasingly understood. Enormous division and inequality sit behind a nation fronted by an enormous economic centre in its capital – one which raises the costs of living and drains policy attention and resources from the country's urban hinterlands. We realise, too late perhaps, that we can appear to be rich at the level of the nation while allowing egregious and dehumanising conditions in so many other parts of our country.

Today there is a hunger for forms of investment and measurement better able to capture our cities' human and environmental needs and to respond to the real richness and potential of community life. This means that measures of wealth and value will need to be better devised and more closely calibrated to more authentic forms of human need and capability, and in recognition that humans exist within bounded ecological relationships with other species and with the resources that give life to our planet. We cannot keep having more in a growth economy that is fixed upon, yet blind to, its catastrophic endpoint. John Lanchester's novel, *The Wall*, in which the young cynically patrol an enveloping boundary to repel climate change fleeing Others, feels too close for comfort. We are but a heartbeat from the realisation not only of a more terminal and depressed urban system but also of a bleak relationship with other urban centres and more vulnerable populations globally. Not only will the UK's city system be at the forefront of these changes, its inequalities will likely begin to reveal in much sharper relief the exit of its affluent minority from degraded public domains to gated communities and leafier suburbs and exurbs, defined by the ability to evade the consequences of declining public investment and its casualties, as well as the increasing imprint of environmental change.

Cities are too important to be left to central government, but in the United Kingdom they are too vulnerable to stand without it, and their diverse and energetic communities have a wealth of creativity and determination to offer that too often is absorbed simply in trying to get by. A balance must be struck in which a more engaged and listening frame of policymaking works in sympathy and with the mutual support of cities and communities. Urban life is far too important for, yet also vulnerable to, a partisan politics. The dramatic spatial inequalities of the United Kingdom are emphasised in our towns and cities and it is here that good and concerted work must be done in concert with urban residents in ways that build stronger, healthier, more cohesive communities under much stronger principles of common participation, mutual listening and social justice.

Together the contributors to this book offer the beginnings of a comprehensive agenda for change. This is just a starting point: genuine engagement with those who are working for change and justice in our cities will put flesh and muscle on the bones of these action points. The policy manifesto on the following pages distils the key ideas and demands of our contributors and shows where any serious urban policy needs to begin.

Chapter 12

A MANIFESTO FOR URBAN POLICY

This book has brought together 23 contributors, with interests spanning a wide range of contemporary policy challenges. Here we bring their ideas together and summarise them in an action list for urban policy, highlighting who should take the lead on what in order to make a real and rapid difference in our cities. This list reflects the contributors' priorities and inevitably there are some gaps; nonetheless it shows there is no shortage of far-reaching but implementable ideas that national and local politicians and policymakers must take seriously.

Individuals, community groups, NGOs, councillors, planners and city governors will all find, we hope, some inspiration from this compilation of the proposals found across this volume. We clearly feel that the greatest resource base, skill sets and capacity to arbitrate, intervene and promote better outcomes can only come through the actions of an engaged, emboldened and better resourced public sector, whether this be at the national, regional or city scales. This is not enough on its own: it also requires engagement on equal terms with citizens who are taking action to support their communities and neighbourhoods. Too often, though, the language of 'empowerment' is used as cover for the offloading of responsibilities. Real empowerment, we suggest, comes when the public sector is both stronger and more responsive, acting as a champion and supporter of its citizens.

Actions for Central Government

1. Replace the objective of economic growth with the objective of growing social capital across government policy.
2. Put sustainability at the heart of policymaking and assess all policies against social outcomes.
3. Develop a cross-government plan to ensure everyone has access to good food and nobody goes to bed hungry, with a clear target of halving household food insecurity by 2025 and a goal of zero hunger in the United Kingdom within ten years.

4. Understand how community well-being can be supported through policy, and enact supporting policies.
5. Undertake concerted public investment in housing. Instead of spending billions on helping existing homebuyers, a significant switch should be made to commit to a 20-year programme to build 3.1 million homes for social rent, including 100,000 new council homes a year.
6. Tackle structural inequalities, recognising that quality of life is unevenly distributed along racial lines and affirming the human rights of people who live in polluted areas.
7. Ensure the education system and national curriculum teaches the dangers of urban pollution and informs urban citizens of their rights not to live in polluted environments. Invest NHS funds in promoting solutions to problems of poor air quality.
8. Reinvest in local and national services. This is needed to manage, respond to and prevent violence in cities, redressing the impact of budget cuts which have had a lasting impact on charities for the homeless, women's refuges, community centres, and police, probation and prisons.
9. Remove the Local Housing Allowance (LHA) cap for people living in private rented housing, which will not only ensure that the benefit adequately covers rent but will prevent discrimination by private landlords against people receiving LHA.
10. Develop a more effective regulatory regime for all landlords.
11. Provide funding to help revive independent tenant organisations to improve community participation and cohesion.
12. Provide local authorities with adequate funding to provide independent housing and necessary social support through Housing First and similarly successful local programmes.
13. Reform private renting by introducing rent control and scrapping 'no-fault' evictions.
14. Develop overarching national policies that prioritise young people, such as the Well-being of Future Generations (Wales) Act 2015.
15. Introduce a Community Right to Buy to give communities first refusal when a piece of land is put on the market, and to buy land that is abandoned, neglected or causing harm to the environmental well-being of the community.
16. Reverse all funding cuts for green and open spaces and restore local planning authorities' financial stability and their ability to spend on landscape projects.
17. Legislate for green infrastructure to be required in all new and retrofitted development, and allow planning authorities to legally challenge developers who attempt to dodge their environmental responsibilities.

18. Planning laws should make preserving and enhancing biodiversity and bioabundance an obligation.
19. Match capital funding with revenue funding across government programmes wherever possible, ensuring that investment in improvements to places also includes investment in the people who will look after those places in the future and bring them to life.
20. Test ways to couple universal basic services with a new Universal Basic Income. Give citizens more say in the services they receive by financing them to make their own choices about how they work while providing the stability of a guaranteed level of basic services.
21. Begin a consistent and comprehensive devolution of powers and resources to cities and localities in order to make elected representatives accountable to their local constituents and responsive to their needs.
22. Give new parents the best start by reintroducing critical services and integrating measures that help support and integrate new parents and improve health and education outcomes (building on the experience of Sure Start).
23. Legislate to help retain public land for public use and the common good in perpetuity by maintaining the freehold of land in public ownership to protect council estates against privatisation, and retain public land for council house building.
24. Devise national policies to fully support Community Land Trusts – allowing us to work around the dominance of profit motives by taking property and land out of the market.
25. Reform national taxation of property to take into account actual values and develop new legislation on land value capture that enables local communities to recover and reinvest land value increases for public benefit.
26. Develop national and regional land-use strategies to include green belts and their use as food production spaces, encouraging and incentivising uses and forms of management that put local people in control and meet local needs.

Actions for National Public Services and NGOs

27. Create an Incredible Edible Health Service, with community kitchens in health centres and edible landscaping in hospitals.
28. Make environmental education and championing a key element of all public sector work/funding, and legislate to move private business into more ecologically sustainable practices.
29. Embed tackling inequality into the work of public agencies by implementing the socio-economic duty established in the 2010 Equality

Act, to ensure that strategic decisions take account of the need to reduce inequalities in outcome that derive from socio-economic disadvantage.

30. Test more innovative approaches to unlock private capital for local social good, alongside government funding programmes that actively pursue best practice based on evidence and experience.

Actions for Urban Leaders – Mayors, Councillors and Chief Officers

31. Design and implement a strategy to end the need for food banks, working with third-sector and community organisations to ensure that people experiencing financial crisis have appropriate advice and cash entitlements.
32. Introduce a right to public space, a shared set of rights of access to, and use of, public open space that apply whoever owns it.
33. Fully implement the real Living Wage for all local authority staff and ensure that all who provide council services are paid the real Living Wage, including care workers, school staff and waste collection workers.
34. Put people at the heart of place stewardship and involve them in the co-production of new projects and the management and maintenance of their local environments.
35. Create 'place directorates', removing silos within local authorities and rebuilding officer teams around balanced placemaking principles and a social ethos.
36. Encourage diversity in 'White spaces', ensuring that urban green spaces are open and welcoming to all.
37. Create an edible public realm, handing over areas of public land to community groups to grow and share food.
38. Plan for food growing in new developments, adopting the Garden City principle of space for food growing around homes.
39. Focus local authority land management on maximising biodiversity and bioabundance, ensuring that it is only damaged when absolutely necessary, and boosted whenever possible.
40. Local authorities should promote active transport (walking and cycling), public transport (including free buses) and provision of car clubs, and they should open up the streets and public parking spaces freed up by such policies for community uses such as playgrounds, food-growing, tree-planting and socialising.
41. Establish Citizens' Assemblies in towns and cities to discuss and agree priorities for the future of council services and how they should be funded. These can work alongside elected local politicians in making decisions about urban affairs.

42. Encourage and support local Fairness Commissions in each town and city to ensure that public services benefit those who most need support and to identify innovations.
43. Enrich social infrastructure, investing in the community-based networks and organisations that provide social support and take the pressure off frontline services.
44. Promote active citizenship through access to information, social networking and developing civic capacities. Urban government should support local citizens to build their own agency so that they can actively make changes in their lives and their neighbourhoods.
45. Encourage values-based collaborations with the full participation of councillors and officers where invited. Their focus and purpose should be decided democratically and reported regularly to full council meetings in public.

Ideas for Cities – Mayors, Community Leaders

46. Listen to families and communities by encouraging the active participation of local communities in decision-making about the solutions and perceived obstacles to reducing violence. Fund relevant services sufficiently to enable them to support and empower local communities to participate in debates on violence in cities.
47. Develop collaborative partnerships and integrate them into public policy through a network of agencies working collaboratively. Address violence holistically through joint working by support services in housing, education, family, employment and health using shared agendas and approaches.
48. Citizens, including those under voting age, need to have genuine political power – in a democracy everyone should matter politically. Citizens' Assemblies and similar projects should be encouraged with a particular role for young people to show they count.
49. At the city/neighbourhood level we should develop schemes to support young people to design new community spaces, and also to build them, power tools and all. Finding small pots of cash to invest in these kinds of projects could pay real dividends.

Actions for Community Groups and Neighbourhoods

50. Develop grassroots alliances to tackle poverty and food insecurity. Support people with lived experience of food poverty to take on governance roles.
51. Shift the focus of help for people experiencing food poverty away from emergency food aid towards approaches that tackle the underlying drivers of poverty.

52. All who work with people experiencing food poverty should affirm the dignity and equality of people who are going hungry.

Action at the Level of the Individual

53. Individuals can make a massive difference to local urban environments by choosing public over private transport, reducing plastic consumption and assisting in local ecological and conservation projects.
54. Vote, participate, act and generally get involved!

CONTRIBUTORS

Rowland Atkinson is Research Chair in Inclusive Societies at the University of Sheffield. He is author of numerous books and papers, including *Alpha City*, *Domestic Fortress* (with Sarah Blandy) and *Urban Criminology* (with Gareth Millington).

Natalie Bennett is a member of the House of Lords and former leader of the Green Party in England and Wales.

Luke Billingham is a youth and community worker at Hackney Quest in North East London, and Head of Strategy at Reach Children's Hub, Feltham.

Emma Bimpson is a research associate at the Centre for Regional Economic and Social Research at Sheffield Hallam University.

Elizabeth Cook is a research fellow at the Centre for Criminology at the University of Oxford.

Niall Cooper is the director of Church Action on Poverty.

Rhiannon Corcoran is a professor of psychology and public mental health at the University of Liverpool.

Simin Davoudi is a professor of environment and planning and director of the Global Urban Research Unit at Newcastle University.

Julian Dobson co-founded the community regeneration magazine *New Start* and is author of *How to Save Our Town Centres*.

Anthony Ellis is a lecturer in sociology and criminology at the University of Salford, Manchester.

Richard Goulding is an urban geographer and writer on housing and financialisation.

Annette Hastings is a professor of urban studies at the University of Glasgow.

Keir Irwin-Rogers is a lecturer in criminology at the Open University and lead criminologist to the cross-party Youth Violence Commission.

Loretta Lees is a professor of human geography at the University of Leicester.

Graham Marshall is director of the urban design practice Prosocial Place and honorary senior research fellow at the Institute of Population Health Sciences, University of Liverpool.

Ian Mell is a senior lecturer in environmental and landscape planning at the University of Manchester.

Madeleine Power is an ESRC postdoctoral fellow at the University of York. She is founder of the York Food Justice Alliance, and Co-Chair of the Independent Food Aid Network.

Glyn Robbins is a housing worker, campaigner and visiting fellow at the London School of Economics.

Jess Steele OBE is an independent community activist and entrepreneur, director of Jericho Road Solutions and a founder trustee of Heart of Hastings CLT.

Kate Swade is co-executive director of Shared Assets CIC which exists to support the use of land for the common good.

Bethany Thompson is a researcher in health and population at King's College London, and was previously a health researcher at the National Centre for Social Research.

Mark Walton is a co-executive director of Shared Assets CIC.

Pam Warhurst is a founder of Incredible Edible Todmorden and the Incredible Edible Network.

INDEX

accumulative dispossession 88
agency gap 119
air pollution 7–8, 63
  asthma from 65
  diseases from 64–65
  impact on health services 65–67
  manmade 65
  NO_2 64, 84
  road transport and 64, 84
  schools 76
air quality, public health and 7, 63
  Black communities and 63–65
  impact on health services 65–67
    human rights 67
    structural inequalities 66
    'White spaces' 66–67
  racial and social inequalities 63–65
algal blooms 84
anxiety, urban 13–14, 38, 43–48
  place stewardship and 46
  transport planning and 46
Arena, John 30
asthma 64–65
austerity 77, 79–82, 117

Bedroom Tax 25
Benefit Cap 25
Big Society 108, 115, 124
bioabundance 81–82
biodiversity 81
British Social Attitudes (BSA) 114
Buurtzorg model of social care 61

Cameron, David 25, 108
Campaign to Protect Rural England (CPRE) 98

Chartered Institute of Environmental Health 108
childhood, mental distress in 41–42
child poverty 13
Cities for the Many, Not the Few 92
Citizens' Assemblies 132
climate poverty 76
CLTs. *See* Community Land Trusts (CLTs)
communities
  assets 8
  food 69
    growing 96
    providers 19
  of interest 40–41
  involvement 40–41
  loss of 8
  well-being 40
Community Land Trusts (CLTs) 90–91, 96, 123, 131
Community Right to Buy 98, 130
cooking skills 69–70
Corporate Social Responsibility (CSR) programmes 78
council services 104–5
Council Tax 12–13
Countryside and Rights of Way Act (2000) 77
COVID-19 pandemic 1–2
Crown Prosecution Service 50
CtrlShift 97

democracy 113–18
  frustrations with 114–15
  hope/despair, source of 113–14, 116–17
  localism 115–16
  politics of 117–18

depression 38
Dignity in Practice project 19
displacement 93–98
Dorling, Danny 52

ecological crisis 2–3
End Hunger UK campaign 15, 20–21
entitativity 38
environmental injustices 64–65
environmental racism 64
Environment Bill (2019) 79
Equality Act (2010) 106
Every Egg Matters campaign 70
exploitation 44–45

Fabian Commission on Food and
     Poverty 18
Fairness Commissions 105, 143
financialisation 24–25, 27
food 69–70
Food and Agriculture Organisation (FAO) 11
food banks 5, 11–15
food deserts 18
food poverty 5
   challenges 18–19
   civil society response to 14–15
   End Hunger UK campaign 20–21
   food aid 15
   food banks 5, 11–15
   government policies on 13–15, 20–22
   Local Pantries for 19
   campaign on 15
   two-child limit and 13
   in unemployed/lowest-income people 12
   working-age social security, cuts in 12–13
Food Power programme 15, 19
Food Standards Agency 11
Fox Gardens council estate,
     Islington 30–33

George, Henry 122–23
Granby 4
Streets project 27, 123
Gray, Thomas 43
Greater London Council (GLC) 30
green infrastructure, in cities 75–80, 94
   austerity programmes and 77, 79–82
   benefits of 75–76, 82
   decline, impacts of 76, 81–82

funding for 77–79
as havens 81–85
management 78–79
parks 75–76
planning 85
guerrilla gardening 77

habitat 45
Hardy, Thomas 43
Harvey, David 124
Hastings 123–24
Healey, John 91
health inequality 76
healthy food 7
Healthy Start, public health initiative 19
Healthy Urban Microbiome Initiative
     (HUMI) 81
Heeley Park project 77–78
Homebaked project 27
Homelessness Reduction Act (2018) 26
Homes for All alliance 34
housing
   allowance 25
   benefit 25
   costs 25
   council 29–35
   council housing, urban 29–35
      change, agenda for 33–35
      people/cities, effects on 29–32
   insecurity 5–6, 8, 23–25, 27–31
      private landlordism and 27
      speculation and 23–24
   investment in 23–24
   private markets 26–27
   private rented sector (PRS) 25–27
   real estate markets 23–25
   self-help 27–28
   social 25–26
   temporary 26
   as tradeable asset 24
   value of 27
Housing and Planning Act (2016) 33
'Housing First' pilots 28
Housing Market Renewal Programme
     109, 119
human rights 67
HUMI. *See* Healthy Urban Microbiome
     Initiative (HUMI)
hunger 7, 12, 17–22

INDEX

Incredible Edible 8, 68–73, 77, 84, 131
Independent Food Aid Network 11, 15, 18, 20
Institute for Fiscal Studies 14

Johnson, Boris 50
Joseph Rowntree Foundation 12, 17

Khan, Sadiq 34

Lanchester, John 128
land 93–98
   disconnection 94–95
   investments in 93–94
Land Compensation Act (1961) 91
Land Justice Network 97
libraries 107
light pollution 84
local housing allowance (LHA) 25, 130
localism 115–16, 117
   efficiency 116
   fairness 116
Localism Act (2011) 75, 98
Local Pantries, for food poverty/insecurity crisis 19
Local Planning Authorities (LPAs) 75–76
London 7–8, 30–32, 34, 63–64, 75–77, 82, 87–90, 93–98
Lost Arts programme 69
LPAs. *See* Local Planning Authorities (LPAs)

Massey, Doreen 4
mattering, violence in city and 55–61
May, Theresa 12
McCartney, Garry 107
Mead, Margaret 73
mental distress 39, 41–42
Menu for Change 15

National Health Service (NHS) 105
National Parks and Access to the Countryside Act (1949) 77
NHS. *See* National Health Service
nihilism 58–59
nitrates 84
nitrogen dioxide (NO_2) 64
noise pollution 84
Northern Distributor Road 38

parks 75–76
Pen Green, in Corby 61
place stewardship 46
Plantlife, environmental charity 82
polis 113
Power, Madeleine 7, 20
precarity 4–6, 26–28
   physical environment and 5
Preston Model 96
private landlordism 27
Privately Owned Public Spaces (POPS) 98
private rented sector (PRS) 25–27
public health challenges 7–8
public services 8, 101–6
   changes in 110–12
      green spaces 110
      local services, rebuilding of 110–11
      universal services 111–12
   commissioners 108
   community centres 107–8
   council services 104–5
   deterioration of 107–8
   Fairness Commissions 105
   inequality 106
   libraries 107
Public Space Protection Orders (PSPOs) 26

Real Estate Investment Trusts 24
rent gap 119
Right to Buy (RTB) 25, 31
rough sleeping, cities 26
Round, Katherine 39
Roy, Arundhati 2

Scotland 106
self-help housing 27–28
self-renovating neighbourhoods 123–24
Sheffield 76–77, 82–84
social bonds 8
social capital 38, 40
social housing 25–26
social inequalities 3, 64–65
Social Market Foundation 17–18
social networks 7
socio-economic duty 106
Solnit, Rebecca 4

Steele, Jess 91
Stephens, Debbie 107
structural inequalities 66
Sustain 15

temporary housing 26
Tenant Management Organisation (TMO) 32–33
tenant unions 27
Trussell Trust 11, 13–16, 18, 20, 22n1
Turner, Ted 32
two-child limit 13

Unison, public services union 108
Universal Basic Income 59–60, 111
Universal Credit system 13, 25
urban democracy 8
urban dispossession
    land
        common good, building 95–97
        Community Right to Buy 98
        displacement 94–98
        national/regional use strategies 97
        right to public space 98
    through gentrification 87–98
urban government 119–24
    change, agenda for 124
    decision-making 121–23
    and destruction of places 119–21
    Granby 4 Streets 123
    Hastings 123–24
Urbanicity Effect 45
urban policy 129–34
    central government, actions for 129–31
    cities, ideas for 133
    community groups/neighbourhoods, actions for 133–34
    individual, actions for 134
    National Public Services, actions for 131–32
    NGOs, actions for 131–32
    urban leaders, actions for 132–33

urban stress 3–4, 38–48
    community well-being and 40
    environments and 39–40
    community involvement and 40–41
    mental distress, in childhood 41–42
urban violence. *See* violence

Vagrancy Act (1824) 26
violence, in city 6–7, 49–61
    acts *vs.* processes 51–52
    crime 49–50
    distribution 49–51
    increase in 49–50, 52
    inequality and 52
    neighbourhoods 49
    physical acts of 52
    response to 52–54
        collaborative partnerships and integration into public policy 53–54
        democratic decision-making, participation of families/local communities 53–54
        local and national services, economic reinvestment in 53
    understanding 51–52
voucher system, for food 15

Wall, The (Lanchester) 128
wealth inequality 2–3
well-being 44
Well-being of Future Generations Act 42, 130
'we-ness' 38–48
White Collar Factory 31–32
'White spaces' 66–67
Wigan Deal 121
Williams, Raymond 44
Winter Garden 123
working-age social security 12–13

Your Local Pantry network 19

zero-hour contracts 88

www.ingramcontent.com/pod-product-compliance
Lightning Source LLC
Chambersburg PA
CBHW021833300426
44114CB00009BA/419